D0431195

"Loving, caring, and careful, this is a wonderfully practical book for every-one. Sooner or later we all have to manage the process of approaching death – either our own or our loved ones. This single compassionate book will take you through everything you need to know. The highest praise I can give is that I will use it myself. So thank you, Jane. I am grateful."

— **WILLIAM BLOOM**, author of *The Power of Modern Spirituality*,
The Endorphin Effect, and *Psychic Protection*, **http://williambloom.com**

"Jane has produced nothing less than a work of true art in completing this guidebook, *Before I Go*. Those of us who work in the field of death and dying have been waiting for such a comprehensive, passionate, resourceful, and thoroughly researched manual. I trust this book because I trust the authenticity of its author. Jane's own face-to-face experiences with death when her beloved Philip died show us that she knows well the places of rawness in the human heart. I trust Jane as a companion for mine and will recommend this book to friends and students alike. And having listened to Jane's advice I have decided, "before I go" I will plan my own happy death!"

— **PHYLLIDA ANAM-AIRE**, author of *A Celtic Book of Dying*,
Celtic Wisdom and Contemporary Living, and *Let Love Heal*

"From spiritual seekers to pragmatists like me, there will be something for everyone in Jane's book. It will help those who've done a journey of loss and grief, those whose health signals a predictable trajectory, and those who are hail and hearty and just want to be prepared, whatever the future holds. I feel I can confidently guarantee that whoever you are, wherever you're coming from, you will find something in Jane's words of wisdom that resonate, and you'll find yourself thinking: 'Aha, that's why I'm reading this book.'"

— **BARBARA CHALMERS**, founder of Final Fling
and author of *Too Busy To Die?*

"As doctors, we say 'prevention is better than cure'. Jane's approach to end of life is very positive. She provides all the tools for a plan which can be easily accessed at the time of death by any member of the family. Because it has been taken care of many months before, there are no surprises, so loved ones feel the immediate benefit and can go forward with confidence knowing what was wanted, even just by doing the 'How Prepared Are You?' quiz. I say, 'prevent the pain with the plan.'"

— **DR. DOREEN MILLER**, author of *The Healthy Business Bridge*, www.themillerhealthexperience.com

"Without Jane's help, we wouldn't have done anything other than a will and some financial information; and we'd have been much less organized. Through our work with her, and the very useful discussions and information, we got clear about what we wanted and didn't want and wrote it down. Jane had a gift for getting us disciplined in a very supportive way, and working together as a couple doing this has made us realize how invaluable it has been."

— **DELCIA MCNEIL**, author of *Bodywork Therapies for Women*, and **RUSSELL MCNEIL**, registered homeopath

"This is a way to bring the many facets of planning for end of life into one place. There are so many things to think about, and also the ones you don't know to think about! Jane's approach for planning and her style of conversation and gentle prodding make it much easier to think about the 'how' of planning for end of life, no matter what stage you're in. While I plan with my mother, I am also having conversations with my husband. As we get older our plan will change, but we do now have a plan and know what the other wants."

— **MARY VARGAS**, founder of Achieve Consulting Group, LCC

"For anyone who has a blended family or has been remarried, this course and workbook is a MUST! Having the excuse that I had an assignment from Jane's course made it easy to open the conversation with my husband, when previously I could not hold his attention for 15 minutes on this topic. And now I feel like I have created a 'living document,' not a 'death document.'"

— **PATTY BURGESS BRECHT**, president of Possibility, www.teachingtransitions.com, www.doingdeathdifferently.com

"Being on the course drove home how much this service is needed; I simply would not do this without handholding. The gap between thinking about it and actually doing it was made blazingly apparent."

— **MYSTE ANDERSON**, founder of Bittersweet Blessing, www.bittersweetblessing.com

Before I Go

The
ESSENTIAL GUIDE *to*
CREATING *a* GOOD
END *of* LIFE PLAN

JANE DUNCAN ROGERS

FINDHORN PRESS

Findhorn Press
One Park Street
Rochester, Vermont 05767
www.findhornpress.com

Text stock is SFI certified

Findhorn Press is a division of Inner Traditions International

Copyright © 2018 by Jane Duncan Rogers

All rights reserved. No part of this book may be reproduced or utilized in any form
or by any means, electronic or mechanical, including photocopying, recording, or by
any information storage and retrieval system, without permission in writing from the
publisher.

Disclaimer

The information in this book is given in good faith and is neither intended to diagnose
any physical or mental condition nor to serve as a substitute for informed medical
advice or care. Please contact your health professional for medical advice and treatment.
Neither author nor publisher can be held liable by any person for any loss or damage
whatsoever which may arise from the use of this book or any of the information therein.

A CIP record for this title is available from the Library of Congress

ISBN 978-1-84409-750-0 (print)
ISBN 978-1-84409-764-7 (ebook)

Printed and bound in the United States by Lake Book Manufacturing Inc.
The text stock is SFI certified. The Sustainable Forestry Initiative® program promotes
sustainable forest management.

10 9 8 7 6 5 4 3 2 1

Edited by Michael Hawkins
Artwork by Jane Duncan Rogers
Text design, layout and graphics (pp. 67 & 162) by Damian Keenan
This book was typeset in Minion Pro and Calluna Sans with Antonio used as a display
typeface.

To send correspondence to the author of this book, mail a first-class letter to the
author c/o Inner Traditions • Bear & Company, One Park Street, Rochester, VT 05767,
and we will forward the communication, or contact the author directly at
https://beforeigosolutions.com

Dedication

· · · · · ·

*This book is dedicated with gratitude
to my husband Philip Rogers,
27.11.45 – 1.11.2011.*

*Without his life and death,
none of what* Before I Go Solutions®
now offers would be possible.

Contents

• • • • • •

How to Use This Guide

••••••

There are two parts to this guide:

SECTION 1: Preparation

SECTION 2: Taking Action

For those who like to jump in and act, you do not need to read the Preparation section. While it is full of interesting, useful and relevant information, and you may very well learn things you didn't know, the main purpose of this Guide is to help you complete an end of life plan that will work well for you, your family members and also any professionals that may be involved in your last days, and afterwards.

This plan can be completed by taking the actions and advice given in Section 2. If you would like more support with this section, you can get a copy of the *Before I Go Workbook: Practical Questions to Ask and Answer Before You Die,* available at **www.beforeigosolutions.com/workbook,** which outlines over 140 questions, with space for you to add your answers.

In both sections of this Guide, you can just dip in and out as you wish, allowing yourself to be drawn to what interests you in the moment. However, having said that I highly recommend you do actually read it all, as you will more than likely discover things you hadn't thought about, or didn't know you needed to know.

I hope you will feel inspired to take action on the process of creating your end of life plan. If you just read this guide, you'll become much more educated, but it will make no difference whatsoever to your own end of life process unless you also answer the questions, communicate about them, and write the answers down. Believe it or not, it is a process that can be enjoyed!

You'll end up with the peace of mind and relief that comes to you (and your family) when you have taken care of these things. You'll then experience the energy release that happens as a result of this, when space in your head is no longer taken up with thinking you really ought to get around to it.

To this end, you might want to get some or all of your family members together to start to talk about end of life matters, and you can use the topics in this book to start an ongoing conversation. Remember, it is possible to enjoy this. One of the *Before I Go* workshop participants said "Brilliant! I never knew speaking about death could be so full of humour." She had been nervous about speaking to her parents about this topic, but was delighted to discover that they were keen to do so. This may sound unusual, but try it – you may be pleasantly surprised.

Introduction

• • • • • •

My husband died in 2011, after just over a year of living with the presence of cancer in our marriage. Having this final year together meant we had an opportunity to deepen our love for each other, make sure there was nothing left unsaid between us, and then get on with living as best we could while he was still healthy enough for that. It was a very precious 14 months for us both, and I've written about it in detail in my book *Gifted By Grief: A True Story of Cancer, Loss and Rebirth.* You can read more about this at **www.giftedbygrief.com**

In Chapter 10, published three years after Philip died, I wrote about some particular life issues we had examined while he was still alive. Our friend Barbara in Los Angeles had emailed with a long list of questions, insisting we answer them before it was too late. After about the third email along the same lines, I spoke to Philip about what we were then referring to as The List (of questions). Here's an extract from that chapter in the book:

> "Come on, we're going to do The List properly now." He was still reluctant, but, lying in bed, with me and the laptop next to him, he didn't have a chance. "It's going to make a huge difference to me in the future, darling, and besides, Barbara will just nag us if we don't."
>
> "Yeah, all right then."
>
> Poor Philip – for a man afraid of dying, this was an amazing act of courage, another step in the acceptance of what was happening. We began at the beginning, and continued on until the end, referring to it later as our final project together. In those two hours, I asked him the questions, and he gave me his answers. There were all kinds of practical questions, from the most basic such as, "What kind of coffin do you want?" to which he replied, "Any old box will do" to more sensitive ones, such as, "Are there any of your personal items you would like to leave to anyone in particular?" This one we discussed in more detail.

It was tough; these are difficult questions to ask of somebody who knows he is going to be dying sooner than later. Feeling a great sense of achievement afterwards, we were very close, connected and loving for the rest of that weekend. Who would have thought that? It ended up being a couple of hours of slightly macabre enjoyment.

Many people contacted me about this chapter in the book, saying what a very good idea it was to answer these questions, but also lamenting the fact they were not getting around to it themselves. Thus the idea of bringing the questions to many more readers was born. By January 2016 I had researched and compiled what was then called *The Good Death Guide: 27 Questions to Ask and Answer Before You Die.* I offered to run a local group to enable people to complete this workbook, and it sold out with a long waiting list. It seemed I had hit on something important. After further revisions, research and more courses, this product became the workbook *Before I Go: Practical Questions to Ask and Answer Before You Die,* and my life started to change. Whereas before I had been working as a life, death and small business coach, now I was focusing on my first love, running groups.

I'd originally trained in 1990 with Louise L. Hay, author of the famous book *You Can Heal Your Life,* and founder of Hay House Publishing. I was the first woman in Europe to offer study groups based on her book, which I did for about ten years or so. It was during this time that I also trained in counselling, and began a private practice in Oxford, England. I also ran a large complementary health clinic during these years. It was only with a move to Scotland in 2007 that I morphed into coaching. Now, with founding the not-for-profit organization *Before I Go Solutions* ®, all my skills are coming together, as I encourage people to face up to what can be a difficult and emotional topic – the fact that they are going to die one day.

It is very easy to talk the talk and not actually walk the walk. It's so easy, that only 23% of people have actually written anything down about their end of life care, despite 82% of people in USA[1] (and similar figures in the UK) saying that getting your affairs in order in this way is a good idea. One of the reasons for this is because it can be an emotional subject. Trying to make practical decisions with the backdrop of you or a loved one being no longer around means it is quite possible you will feel like giving up, putting it off, be overwhelmed or exhausted by the whole process. Not to mention perhaps feeling tearful.

However, the process also brings black humour, giggles, and paradoxically is very life-affirming. There's nothing like a little humour to lighten what is potentially a charged situation. For instance, a family member, upon hearing that my husband had stomach cancer, said, "Well, think of it this way - at least the food bills will go down." Some might find that offensive, but Philip and I thought it hilarious, and recognized it for what it was – an attempt to lighten a potentially very heavy conversation. Right here, right now, when it is so obvious that you are very much alive, it really is possible to contemplate the end of you or your loved ones' lives. A participant in one of the *Before I Go* groups said:

> "On an emotional level, this class helped me feel so grateful for my life, the people in it, and the choices I get to make. On a practical level, I was helped to prepare the legal and personal documents that will make dying and death easier on myself and my family. And you know what? The class was FUN. It was life affirming and joyful. Don't be afraid to talk about death; it just may bring you to life!"
>
> — Sherry Richert Belul, USA

What also happens when we begin to think about death is that we naturally start to contemplate the kind of life we are currently living. They go hand in hand, even though we may pretend they don't. You can see this really easily when someone has a near miss in an accident; or is diagnosed with a life-threatening illness; or knows someone who died or nearly died. It stops us in our tracks and we get to reflect on what is important to us while we are alive. Death, while it can hit with the force of a sledgehammer, is a very tender subject.

We need to be kind and careful with ourselves and others when we discuss anything to do with end of life matters. It's important to be as non-judgmental as possible; everyone deals with this in their own way, even the fifty-year-old man who told me the other day that his thirty-year-old son was asking him to sort out his affairs and let him know where bank details and other documents were in his apartment. The father told me he wasn't going to do that because he didn't want to think about death, and anyway, he wasn't going to die! Even this kind of blanket statement has its place – as the famous saying goes, you can lead a horse to water but you can't make it drink.

So where are you with this? Are you being reluctantly led to the water? Are you poised at the water trough, afraid of what the water might contain? Are you sniffing the surface of it? Have you taken a sip, only to have backed off? Or are you drinking slowly and steadily? There is room for all of this, and I encourage you to move forward step by step, a little bit each day, or each week. Here are some tips to make it easier:

- Make good use of the Resources at the end of the Guide.
- Set aside some time in your diary to focus on a particular chapter or section in the Guide.
- Make a commitment to yourself to get this done, bit by bit.
- Buddy up with someone else to make the process easier.
- Join the *Before I Go* Facebook group for support and encouragement – **www.facebook.com/groups/beforeIgo/**
- Join a *Before I Go* course — **www.beforeigosolutions.com**

Join me in helping to bring about my vision of having people the world over become more at ease with talking about dying, death and grief; of having them able to talk over the dinner table about all matters of life and death; to bring death into life once more.

Discover the relief and peace of mind that reading this Guide and completing the questions brings you. This is arguably the greatest gift you can give those left behind.

"A good end of life plan is a great going away present."

— JD-R

SECTION ONE

......

PREPARATION

1

Why Now?

● ● ● ● ● ●

"Unless the mind frees itself from fear,
there is no possibility of understanding the extraordinary
strength, beauty and vitality of death."

— JIDDU KRISHNAMURTI, Indian philosopher, 1895-1986

As the baby boom generation (those born between 1946-1964) become closer to the end of their lives, they are having to deal not just with age-ing parents, but also the fact that they too have aged. Bones shrink, muscles slacken, wrinkles and grey hairs appear – the body points to what the mind may continue to deny for many years. But the fact of the matter is, your body will end at some point, either slowly or suddenly, or any manner of speed in between.

This generation have typically been one of movers and shakers – living throughout the sixties opened them to a whole different way of life and it is this curiosity, willingness to engage and motivation to take action which is showing up now. Hence the interest in how to approach old age, and a redefining of what that is. Esther Rantzen, famous UK TV personality, said on a recent documentary, *The Baby Boomers' Guide to Growing Old*, that no-one now called themselves old, just 'older'.

Questions are being asked of the medical establishment (and sometimes by those in the medical establishment themselves – see Dr. Atul Gawande's famous book *Being Mortal* in the Resource section for a great discussion on end of life care in the USA). Questions are also being asked of the funeral industry, motivated by prices for funerals continuing to rise - why do we have to have a funeral director at all? Can I take care of the body myself? Why does it cost so much? Must I wear black? Is embalming necessary? Can't I arrange my own funeral? I see all of these as very healthy questions. This is a 'growing market' as the baby boomers begin to come to terms with the fact that they too, are dying off, one by one, and that the costs of getting old are something to be taken into account, along with all the other things that need to be attended to.

In the USA, depending on the retiree's age, health condition, and expected lifetime, estimated future healthcare needs vary but are predicted to amount to approximately $146,000 for an individual who's 65 years old and has an expected lifetime of 20 years. This includes any costs not paid by Medicare. If the individual lives until she is 90 years old, she will need $220,600 for healthcare costs, and if the retiree is suffering from a chronic condition, such as cancer, expected healthcare costs will undoubtedly surpass $300,000.[2]

In the UK, the estimated cost for just one day of community care at the end of life is £145 compared with the cost of £425 for a specialist palliative in-patient day bed in hospital.

Changing the setting of care for a patient at the end of life has the potential to reduce the daily cost of care by £280. Between 355,000 and 457,000 patients need palliative care every year. If additional community services were developed to enable even 30,000 patients to reduce their hospital stay by just four days, there would be a potential saving of £34 million.[3]

The Medical Model

The current healthcare system in the Western world educates doctors to keep people alive. In fact, doctors cannot do otherwise, for fear of committing an illegal action. It is important to know this, because by addressing what you want at the end of your life, well before you get there, you will optimize being treated in the way you wish. Otherwise you risk doctors and nurses simply doing their job – which is to prolong your life with life-sustaining treatments. This means things such as being resuscitated, given antibiotics for an infection even if you have a terminal illness, and kept alive for months while in a coma – which may be exactly what you want, but what if it isn't? If this is not thought through carefully beforehand and your relatives and doctors know about it, then the likelihood is that your life will be prolonged longer than you would have wished. See page 86 about advance directives for more on this.

Fear Gets in the Way

Statistics show that 100% of us will die. So why is it that only 21% of us are willing to write anything down about our end of life plans? Even a will, arguably the most important document, is only taken care of by about 53% of all adults in the UK (figures are similar in the USA). There's many practical reasons given for not having a will, but underlying it all is often fear. Fear of not existing, of the unknown, of what it actually means to die. Religious fear, fear of what will happen to our family after we've gone, and fear of whatever beliefs we hold coming true. Fear of what happens when you actually die, fear of being in pain: just plain, simple fear.

Taking care of one's end of life in advance means you get to face this fear. Like most fears, it is the fear of the fear itself that is the real problem; many of the *Before I Go* course participants have said that once they started, the fear disappeared. Others found ways to view their life and death differently, so the fear took a back seat. Seeing things through a different lens can be a very powerful way to meet both life and death.

> "I was scared that if I started to address these things, then it would make them happen. Then I realized how superstitious that was, and decided to face up to it instead. I am so relieved, and glad I did it; now I have my son's guardianship taken care of, finally."
>
> — John, Canada

2

The Elephant in the Room

• • • • • •

"Death is not extinguishing the light, it is only putting
out the lamp because the dawn has come."

— **RABINDRANATH TAGORE**, Indian author, 1861-1941

Humans often spend an inordinate amount of time and energy avoiding the fact that there is an elephant in the room. This phrase refers to an important topic which everyone is aware of but which isn't discussed due to the topic being perceived as uncomfortable to talk about. But how on earth did dying and death (and the associated grief) become an elephant? It's not so long ago that (in country areas at least) the deceased were laid out at home, the coffin placed in the front room of the house for viewing, or the body laid in bed, available for whoever wanted to pay their last respects.

Only 50 years or so ago the bereaved wore black armbands for many months, to show they were mourning and needed to be treated more gently, just as we behave towards mothers who are pregnant. As health has improved, however, and as we live longer, in Western society it has become more and more unusual even for middle-aged adults to have seen a dead body. This brings with it a fear of what death actually is, and a general disinclination to admit that it will happen at all. Hence the elephant in the room.

Most of us choose to see only the room, not the elephant in it. Even when it is towering over us, as in being diagnosed with a terminal illness, or a life-limiting disease, many still choose to pretend the elephant doesn't exist. It then befalls to the family and friends left behind to clear up the mess after that person has died. Because an individual's life *is* messy. Just look around you right now, wherever you are. If you had died yesterday, what would your loved ones find (apart from your dead body)? Would they be able to easily tidy things up? Would they need to start a detailed search through mounds of 'stuff' (online and offline) for important documents? Could they easily find your list of contacts or address book? Admitting the elephant exists is the first stage in accepting that life includes the end of it too. This is a drawing I spontaneously did when I first realized my work was going to be focused on something that many people didn't want to talk about.

To acknowledge the presence of End of Life Elly, you have to admit an elephant exists in the first place. You can do this right now by simply saying 'hallo' to Elly, out loud. By doing this you are beginning the process of admitting that death happens. We will die. Our family and friends will die. We will feel grief, and they will too when we die. We don't know when it will happen, but it will happen at some point. Once you have said 'hallo', you can turn around and face her with any one of these 3 steps:

1. **Take a walk outside in nature,** and consciously use your five senses as you walk. The walk could be around your garden, a park, a wood; anywhere there are plants, trees, bushes, wildlife. Take 15 minutes on that walk to deliberately look for signs of both life and death. Notice that seedling growing; then notice the dead leaves from earlier that are being ground up into little pieces under your feet. Hear the birdsong. Touch the bark on a tree and notice the texture and how it makes you feel. Pick up a twig or piece of wood. Feel it, while understanding that this is a piece of a larger tree or bush, but it

is 'dead'. Notice any living and dead animals you see. Become aware that life itself includes death, just as death includes life. Contemplate the idea that the body you inhabit is just the same as a tree, plant or animal that dies.

2. **Visualize Elly in your room**, right now. Just see her standing, benignly, in the corner. Imagine saying hallo to her. When you do this you are saying hallo to the presence of death within life. Notice how this makes you feel, and what thoughts you have about it. Have a conversation with her if you feel brave enough – you might find yourself surprised at what she has to say.

3. **Acknowledge that your own death will take place.** Pay attention to how you feel about that. Jot down your thoughts in a journal. If it feels really scary still, then just notice that and leave it for now. You can come back to it later.

"When I start to think about my own death, I feel terrified of not existing. That means I just don't want to look at this kind of end of life stuff at all. And yet I know I have to."

— Michael, England

How Do You Know There Is an Elephant in the Room?

You feel uncomfortable around whatever topic the elephant represents. It's that simple. Everyone will feel it, to a lesser or greater degree, it just depends on how aware you are. Elephants are everywhere, not just to do with death, although that's what we are focusing on here. The other day, I was being interviewed for a place on a business course. I entered a room where there were four other candidates. No-one was speaking and there was an atmosphere of tension in the room. There was definitely an elephant lurking, the one called 'we mustn't talk to each other because we are all competing for a place on the course'. I'm known for addressing elephants, whether they're called End of Life Elly or not. So I started to speak. It took a while, but before long, we were all talking and engaging with each other, and had moved from an atmosphere of competition to one of more relaxation, and hoping the best for everyone. Phew!

What Happens When End of Life Elly Doesn't Get Acknowledged?

Elly doesn't mind if she gets acknowledged or not. The onus is on you to interact with her - she (death) is there, whether you like it or not. However, if she isn't paid attention to, she will cause problems. I mentioned before about the mess that has to be cleared up when someone dies without any of their affairs organized. The way this mess shows up is in administrative muddles, problems with relationships as people adjust to their loved one not being there any more, arguments, long-standing disputes erupting, legal battles, inability to move on, and a lot of time and unnecessary expense being involved.

Think of Prince, the famous pop star, who died suddenly in April 2016. He had not prepared well for a good end of life; hadn't even left a will. Now sorting out his affairs will take the family and solicitors many years, and thousands of dollars, before it is all resolved. Is this really how you want to leave things for your family? You may not be a millionaire but I'm sure you still have treasured possessions. However, even when you have the best of intentions, doing this work takes courage, commitment and confidence. Helping you is what this Guide is about, as is all the work *Before I Go Solutions* ® does.

What Happens after Elly Has Been Acknowledged?

She will no longer be an elephant in the room. Instead, she will become a useful part of the furniture. She doesn't go away, but she certainly won't be causing trouble after your family member or friend dies; instead she will be a benign presence, just part of life itself. She will enable you to more fully focus on being alive, and gain the most from doing so. She'll encourage an ironic joke or two, or even full-blown laughter. Acknowledging her will also make it easier for you to be around people who are grieving, as well as those who are dying. So go on, have a go – turn round and say hallo by reading this Guide, and reflecting about what comes up for you as you do so.

3

Why Bother?

● ● ● ● ● ●

"Death is not the opposite of life but a part of it."
— **HARUKI MURAKAMI**, Japanese writer, b. 1949

Let's face it, there is never going to be a good time to address anything to do with dying, death or grief. When you're fit and healthy, the last thing on your mind is the end of your life. However, this is actually the very time to take your head out of the sand and admit that life in your body will expire one day, and that you need to address the practical aspects of that. Planning for death when you are healthy means there is a lot less to think about if you become seriously ill.

Anything to do with the ending of life is not an easy thing to contemplate for most people. What *is* easy is doing nothing. Which is why research for Dying Matters in the UK found that:

- Only 36% of people had made a will.
- Only 29% had let someone know their funeral wishes.[4]

In the USA, research according to Gallup in 2016 stated that 44% of all American adults do not have a will. Amongst minorities, the figures are higher.[5] In both countries, that's an awful lot of people who die whose relatives or friends have no idea how they wanted to be treated towards the end of their life. Nor did they know what they would have wanted done with their body, and if they wanted a funeral or not. It's a lot of decision making at a time when your family or friends are already feeling hammered by grief, and likely to be suffering one of its main effects – inability to make decisions easily. For instance, in the UK, only 51% of people with a partner knew what their partners' wishes were for the end of their life. Imagine, your spouse or partner dies and you don't know what they would have wanted, even though you maybe knew them really well, or so you thought. You don't know whether they wanted to be buried or cremated; you don't know what kind of coffin they wanted, or whether they wanted one or not;

you don't know if they even wanted a funeral (it's not compulsory to have one). It's a lot of missing information, and it can cause considerable distress to the one left behind. If you haven't gone through it, it's hard to understand the soothing effect that knowing you are carrying out your partner's wishes can have.

However, many people are, in theory, interested in planning ahead, especially when considering the idea of 'dying well'. Research from a Compassion in Dying report showed that those who had their wishes formally recorded were 41% more likely to be reported as dying well. Further research showed that 82% of people would not want their doctor to make final end of life treatment decisions on their behalf, and 52% would rather make these decisions themselves, with their wishes written out in advance. [6]

When asked, it's clear that most people are interested in planning ahead, at least theoretically. However, the current confusion and lack of awareness amongst both the public and healthcare professionals doesn't help people to prepare well, and can even interfere in them making good end of life plans. This combined with the lack of practical support available to help people complete their plans does not help the situation. Hence the existence of *Before I Go Solutions* ® and the products and programmes on offer.

Here are some of the reasons people have given for completing their end of life plans:

"I wanted to get my affairs in order, so my sons would have an easier task after I'm gone."

– Michael, Scotland

"I don't want anyone to have to deal with what I had to do when my parents died."

– Fiona, Scotland

"When I went home at Thanksgiving this year, my parents asked if they could meet with me and my siblings to talk about their funeral and other plans and wishes. I think they felt good knowing their wishes would be honoured by us and they got it off their chest. It was hard for us but we were glad they wanted us to know and we could hear from them what they wanted. They were a good role model for us all."

– Kathleen, USA

Whatever the motivating reason is, there's no doubt that taking the steps to address the practicalities involved in the end of a life are important. Just as prospective new parents plan for the birth of their baby, so too it benefits everyone involved when you make your end of life plans.

But Plans Never Go to Plan!

'If you want to make God laugh, tell him your plans.' This joke is funny simply because plans so often don't turn out the way you want them to. However, the plan itself is something that gives you (and your family) a sense of security. With that, fear can take a back seat, and when fear is absent, love gets to come forward. In fact, the very act of planning in itself helps the mind to feel calmer about what might happen. A plan also produces organized structures and systems for those left behind, for yourself if you need to find something quickly, and finally, once you've completed your end of life plan, it can be struck off your to-do list and all you need to do then is revisit regularly to make sure it is up to date and reflecting your current wishes.

Wanting to Be in Control

Wanting to be in control of one's end of life is not unusual, especially for those who have seen first-hand how challenging it can be for those who are dying, and their relatives and friends. Many people say they just want nature to take its course, and there is nothing wrong with this. It is a completely personal choice whether you have an end of life plan or not. Some people, having educated themselves or been in the end of life care professions are clear that they do not want to just let nature do its thing. Others are willing to trust that whatever happens, will be acceptable to them. It really doesn't matter, when we are talking about the ending days, weeks or months of your *own* life. What does matter though, is what you leave behind you, because that is what affects others. Regardless of whether you choose to let nature take its course or not towards the end of your life, there will still be the matter of a body to be disposed of and a life to tidy up for those left behind. Taking care of this kind of practical aspect of your life is a great gift to your relatives.

The Derailing Effect of Grief

When you realize how utterly discombobulating grief can be, the motivation to take care of the administrative effects of your life increases dramatically. I was astonished at how little I could do, particularly in the months directly after Philip's death, and at a time when I was being required to make all sorts of decisions. And I was lucky – in the last few months of his life, we had answered that list of questions together. So after he died, I had a document I could view to find out what we had discussed, although I also discovered we had missed loads out. For example, we didn't consider how he might like his body to be transported to the funeral home (at the time, we had no idea there were other ways to take care of bodies than an undertaker or funeral director). Because he died in hospital, his body was brought to the funeral home two hours away by the undertaker. If we had addressed this, we might just have been able to have a friend do it in an estate car, or a white van man pick it up. (I think Philip would have laughed at that; but that's the thing, I didn't know whether he would or not, and so I just went with the status quo, which ended up costing a lot of money.)

It'll Never Happen to Me

This is a common thought, and certainly I used to think that, albeit not very consciously. The fact of the matter is, death *does* happen to people like you and me. It can, and does, happen out of the blue, like a distant cousin of mine who lost control of his car one evening, smashed into a tree, and died at the wheel, aged just 24. Tragic.

A diagnosis of a life-threatening illness can make you stop in your tracks; a gentle but slow demise as your parents age naturally and the body winds down to the end of its life is a more common way that death visits a family. Yes, it is easier to do nothing about end of life planning. Much easier, but here are some of the specifics of what could happen; you may find some of them surprising. (The stories illustrating them are all true examples.)

Seven Reasons to Bother Doing
an End of Life Plan

1. **You fall ill or have an accident, having assumed that your next of kin will be able to take care of you.**

    The term next of kin often means your nearest blood relative. In the case of a married couple or a civil partnership it usually means their husband or wife. However, it is a title that can be given by you to anyone, even friends, and you can name more than one next of kin. Many people assume that having appointed a next of kin, that is who will be able to deal with all your affairs, should you not be able to do so. However, this is not necessarily the case, and will depend on the law in your jurisdiction (see page 82 on power of attorneys). The term 'next of kin' is in fact primarily used for the emergency services to know who to keep informed about your condition and treatment. In the UK, the next of kin has no legal rights, which means that they cannot make decisions on your behalf. In order for them, or anyone else to make decisions for you, they have to have been appointed power of attorney (see point 2 below).

    If this has not already been put in place, no-one can deal with your affairs (either health or financial) without court action to appoint a guardian, which can easily take months to get sorted. The guardian might be someone you wouldn't want, like the local council. Is that really who you would want to be making decisions about you? Also, if a guardian had to be appointed, a lot of your money would be spent unnecessarily on lawyers' fees to set this up.

    Finally, no-one would be able to access information about you, consent to, or refuse medical treatment on your behalf. In the USA, next of kin is a legally defined term, and they may have rights, depending on the individual state law, so be sure to research this for your own state.

"One of the things this process has made me realize is that what I really want to do, in six months to a year, is just have a party! And invite all my family and friends before I die."

— Richard, England

2. **You die with no copy of a last will and testament (or with an out-of-date one).**

    Even if you have a will, if it is out of date, has the wrong name on it, or is in any other way invalid, it will be treated as if there was no will at all. If this happens, then:
    - It will cost more, be more complicated and take much longer than if you have a valid will.
    - Your property may be inherited by someone you are separated from, or their children.
    - If you are living together your partner will not automatically inherit.
    - The government says who gets your property, and the government will eventually inherit if you have no traceable relatives.
    - There is no chance of saving tax.
    - The situation is likely to cause discord and argument in the family.

    "My partner Brodie died after a long illness. We had discussed a will together, but although it had been written to express his wishes that I could live in the house until my death, as we weren't married, the will, although it had been signed, was not witnessed. This caused it to be invalid. Brodie's children, who inherited, gave me notice to move out soon after the funeral, and I lost everything my partner and I had created together."
    – Sile, Scotland

3. **You become seriously ill with no Advance Directive (Living Will/ Advance Decision/Advance Healthcare Plan) instructions to your doctors.**

    An advance directive or decision is a document that states how you wish to be treated if you are incapacitated and cannot convey your own wishes with regard to your medical treatment. It specifically allows you to refer to treatment you do *not* wish to receive. If you don't have one then not only will doctors not know what you might want, those making medical decisions with your doctors might not know either.

    What's more, family members might easily argue over your care and treatment. As a worst-case scenario, you might be kept alive for a long time in a vegetative state, when you might not have wanted that. Ultimately, even if you had a poor quality of life, you may well receive life-prolonging treatment when it is the last thing you would have wanted. (See Page 86)

"My husband Samuel had a massive stroke, and wasn't expected to live. He had not written an advance directive, but despite me and the family stating he would not want to receive any life-prolonging treatment, the hospital proceeded with all kinds of tubes. He did not die, and has improved somewhat, but is still in a state of health that I believe he would have hated. And there is nothing we can do about it."

— MaryAnne, USA

4. **You die with no record of your wishes for after your death.**
    This is a very common state of affairs, and even if you have a will with those wishes in it, that may not be found or read until after the funeral has taken place. It means you are quite likely not to have the funeral you would have wished for, or in the way you would have wished; it may well be that your family argues over your belongings; or that you have a funeral that goes against your religious or spiritual beliefs.

"My friend died just before she could plan for her life savings to go to her two children. But instead of them being the beneficiaries, her second husband took his girlfriend (the one he had before his wife died) for a 6-month long trip around the world with the money."

— Patty, USA

5. **You become unable to communicate through an illness or accident with no record of your wishes made previously.**
    Thus the following are quite possible:
    - You may spend time watching TV/listening to music or radio you really don't like.
    - You don't wear the style of clothes you would choose.
    - You don't get the chance to keep in touch with friends or visit places you enjoy.
    - You don't get the kind of food and drink you enjoy.

"I was visiting my old friend in a nursing home. I knew I might not be recognized, due to her ongoing dementia. But I was really shocked to find her wearing a bright pink jumper; Joan had much preferred subdued pastels, and this shocking pink was simply not in keeping with her personality. I was so cross, I kicked up a fuss, and got Joan into more suitable clothing, but the whole episode left me feeling really shocked and distressed."

— Beth, England

6. **You die without your practical/ financial affairs in order.**
   The amount of time needed to sort out the financial affairs and administration left behind when someone dies can be quite overwhelming. Often, administrative tasks need to happen fairly quickly and at a time when those responsible are still grieving and probably not thinking straight, therefore making it even harder to do. Do you really want to leave this kind of burden for your loved ones? Plus, it is quite possible that expensive assistance may be needed that you did not want, thus leaving less for the family to inherit. This also assumes that the family are in agreement about what happens with inheritance and debts, if any.

   It is alarming how many disputes occur over money after someone has died. If you haven't organized for someone else to access your computer or phone, or you can't access bank accounts for any reason, it may be that money from internet bank accounts won't be claimed and inherited. All of this can cause the family (or friends) much more stress than if you had left them clear instructions in your end of life plan.

7. **You have important information but it isn't all in one place.**
   This makes it much more difficult for your family and/or friends to take care of your affairs after you have died. You risk:
   • Bank accounts never being found, and monies eventually going to the government.
   • Your will not being found and thus your estate gets allocated according to the laws of your country.
   • Those dealing with your affairs finding themselves with much more work to do.

Start as soon as you can, so you are dealing with this topic in a hypothetical way. It's much easier than waiting until you absolutely have to attend to these things. My husband really wasn't that keen on answering any of the questions that I wrote about in *Gifted By Grief*, and he was already in the process of dying. It would have been much easier if we had addressed them before he was even ill.

> "I learned after returning to work a few weeks ago that one of my students had died suddenly while I was away – she was only 48-years old. I understand her family is in turmoil about what to do and this brings home how very important it is that all of us make our plan."
>
> — Janet, USA

There are a lot of reasons to take action on your end of life plan now – which is why you are reading this. So let's get on with it! Turn to the next chapter to begin with understanding how to talk about death. This is really important, as many of the questions around this topic cannot be answered fully without having talked to the various people involved.

4

Talking about Death

● ● ● ● ● ●

"To fear death, my friends, is only to think ourselves wise,
without being wise: for it is to think that we know
what we do not know. For anything that men can tell,
death may be the greatest good that can happen to them:
but they fear it as if they knew quite well that it was
the greatest of evils. And what is this but that shameful
ignorance of thinking that we know what we do not know?"

— **SOCRATES**, Greek philosopher, 469 BC - 399 BC

In the Western world, we are not very good at talking about death. It's almost as if it has become a taboo subject. One of the ways we demonstrate our uncomfortableness on this subject is to use euphemisms for death. They do have their place; it's much better people talk about this subject in euphemisms than not talk about it at all, and sometimes it is just plain sensitive to use a euphemism instead of the bluntness of telling it like it is.

Euphemisms come from all sorts of sources, here's just a few of them:

- Departing, giving up the ghost, loosening the silver cord – the Bible
- Take the ferry – Greek mythology
- Pay one's debt to nature – Latin
- Slip one's cable – from the world of shipping
- Kick the bucket – comes from the livestock industry
- Conk, cop it, falling a victim, shedding one's blood, pushing up the daisies – originated during wartime

Notice the language used the next time someone you know dies. Pay attention to what is being said, and how you feel about it. Are you using a euphemism to avoid the subject? Make a conscious choice to use words that suit you, the person you are referring to, and the situation. In this chapter, you'll find several different ways to introduce (and keep on talking about) a subject most people find challenging, even at the best of times.

Working at a hospice, I asked a woman

What's it like to know that you are dying?

She responded

What's it like pretending that you aren't?

@DeathCafe

© Before I Go Solutions ®

Talking with Doctors and Medical Professionals

'It is crucial!' Many people have asked me whether it is okay to speak to their doctor about their end of life plans, and this is what I say. Some have worries they will be wasting the doctor's time. If that is you, then please know it is more of a waste of doctors and nurses time when they don't know what you want. Book a double appointment, let the receptionist know what you want to discuss at the appointment, or ask for extra time in advance, and take along any preparatory work you have done, and a list of questions (see section on Advance Directives for more information). If you have nothing wrong with you, preface your conversation opener with something like 'I know I'm not ill, but I saw my friend/relative die recently in circumstances that would not have been what I wanted, so I thought I had better do something about it now, as none of us know just when we will die.' Make sure that at least this doctor and the rest in the team know what you want.

For those outside the UK or who have to pay for their medical treatment for any reason, ask your surgery for any protocol they have about this kind of appointment. Remember, money spent now may well save you even more money later.

Another concern is that doctors may themselves feel uncomfortable about talking about dying, especially as their job is to make people better. This is important, because medical professionals are trained to keep us alive and healthy. In future years, medical training may well include more training in palliative and end of life care but for now, it is safer to assume that they will be trained to do what they are required to do legally, which is to provide life-sustaining treatment for as long as is necessary or possible, given the individual situation of the patient.

Talking about a Subject Hardly Anyone Wants to Talk about

Why don't people want to talk about death? There are many reasons for this behaviour, such as:

- They think if they do, it will happen to them quicker
- It makes them realize it will happen to them one day
- It feels horrible/scary/intimidating/perplexing/upsetting/ – any other feeling word you want to use

So if you are going to introduce this topic, it will take some thinking about beforehand. You yourself may not subscribe to any of these reasons above, but you never know how other people might feel. So here are three pointers from the *Before I Go* course in How To Talk About Dying, Death or Grief:

1. **Prepare in Advance**

   What do you need to reflect on before you can even think of having a conversation? Just take a few moments to think about someone with whom you would like to speak on the subject of end of life. There may be more than one person, so think about it separately for each one. Put yourself in their shoes, so you can be as sensitive as possible. Then think about what is important for you about dying, death and grief that you might want to share, and why that is important for you. It might be different for different people. For instance, you or a loved one may be terminally ill; you might just feel strongly about preparing in advance, or be a proponent of assisted dying. You might have recently lost someone very close to you, or you might work in a related field. You might just be the kind of person who knows that what we fear, but then face up to, can bring a kind of liberation that is not only unexpected, but also very freeing.

"I wanted to talk about my spiritual beliefs with my daughter, but I was hesitant as I knew she didn't hold the same beliefs. So I took the time to be more aware of the essence of our beliefs and approached a conversation from that angle, which worked well. We both felt closer afterwards, which was a very pleasant surprise."

— Cynthia, England

Once you've identified a person, the next thing is to consider when and where would be a good time to talk. Sometimes when you're walking alongside one another it's easier to talk about this kind of thing than it is in a face-to-face situation, so choosing your moment on a walk might work for you. If you are sitting around a table it could be over coffee, tea, and cake, as in a Death Cafe (see Resources). It could be over a meal; maybe you even set up a meal with the purpose of talking about this. One of the *Before I Go* course participants invited all her adult children over for Sunday lunch one day with the express purpose of talking about this. They had a family business together, so it was doubly important for them.

"After my aunt died, about six months later I said to my son, 'Remember when Auntie Jeannie died, I was thinking about it the other day and what I realized was she died quite well. It was relatively easy for her. I was thinking how to make it easier for me, when it's my time, and one of the things that would make it easier would be if you'd help me to organize some administrative things now. Would that be okay?' He was a bit taken aback at first, but he knew what I meant about Auntie Jeannie, and agreed to help if he could. I was so glad I had raised the subject, it brought me relief just doing that."

— Susanne, England

Remember that often doing something else, i.e., walking, eating, creating something together can make it much easier to talk about a challenging matter. While normally eye contact is a beneficial thing in any conversation, in this one, it can be more easily done when your eyes only meet occasionally, and on purpose.

Think about where would be a good place for this conversation – a noisy restaurant might not be ideal. Also think about what are the most important things you want to say. If you don't know these in advance, then you may very well miss the opportunity.

2. **Start the Conversation**

   How do you start such a conversation? Some suggestions are below, but use your individual situations. If someone in the area where you live has recently died, that can provide an opener. If you went to a funeral, or are going to a funeral, that can also provide a starting point. Even a celebrity dying can make a conversation about death feel appropriate. For instance, when a famous person dies suddenly, it is quite acceptable to say, 'That makes me think about what I would do in that situation' and lead on from there.

   - Since X died, I've been thinking about life and death a lot. How do you feel about it?
   - What do you think happens after you die?
   - Do you know what you want for your funeral?
   - What do you think a 'good' death might look like?
   - I'd love your help with something...
   - I'd love to talk something through with you; can you be my sounding board?
   - I know you've had some health concerns recently, how has it affected what you think about living a long life?
   - I have some legal matters to sort out, and I need to find a power of attorney. Would you be willing to talk about this with me?
   - I need to think about my future and I also need someone to help me just talk it through. Would you be willing to do that?
   - I've been answering some questions about how I want my end of life to be; I'd like you to see my answers and I'm wondering what your answers would be?
   - Are there any particular milestones you would like to meet? (E.g., an 80th birthday, a grandchild's graduation.... This is especially useful if the person is terminally ill.)

Conversations don't have to be just with family members; you can speak with friends, work colleagues, church companions, group members or anyone at all. Remember you never know how people are going to react until you open the door on the subject. Keep an open heart even if the initial response is not what you would prefer.

3. **Qualities Needed while Having a Conversation**

PATIENCE: The *Before I Go* (BIG) conversation is indeed a big one! Often, time is needed to think, to reflect and to ponder the impact of end of life matters on oneself, but also on others. If you are used to thinking about these matters, be aware that those you are wanting to speak to may never have thought about them. So it is an ongoing conversation, and you don't have to cover everything in one go. That's probably impossible, anyway.

"My husband wouldn't talk to me about anything; I've had such a hard time over the years trying to have these kind of conversations with him. He somehow just never had the time, interestingly. But when I had to do the homework set in the *Before I Go* class, I simply told him my homework was, 'Have a conversation with a close family member', and he agreed to do it. We ended up having an hour and a half of really good, even amusing, conversation about what we were going to do. This was particularly important as we have a blended family, which makes it all the more complicated."

— Patty, USA

LISTENING: While you're having the conversation, remember to listen. Really listen, not just paying apparent attention, while what you are doing is listening to the contents of your own mind. Keep focused on being curious, instead of criticizing or being judgmental. That means keeping an open mind to what you hear, and allowing the other person space to have their opinion – and being prepared to learn, and perhaps change your own mind. Think of the word 'curiosity' - it has an openness and interested tone to it. When you are judgmental you don't have that openness, because you've put the blinkers on and you're only looking right ahead with whatever it is that you're thinking of, and not being interested in anything else.

When that happens, what is heard may be perceived as a threat and you often can't help but open your mouth and out come blaming, defensive words or criticism of the other person or of the situation. That's why I'm saying come to this in an open-hearted way where you don't take things personally. The best way to do that is simply to be curious, as if you were doing research for a project to which you're not attached.

OPENNESS: With these kinds of conversations, you need to be honest, open, and vulnerable yourself. This is one reason why preparation in advance is so important. If you are willing to be and feel vulnerable, you create safe conditions and space for others to be so as well. Remember a saying that was a favourite of my husband's: 'In your vulnerability lies your strength.'

All this means you have to be honest with yourself of course, so do the preparation – answer the questions in this Guide, and begin to demonstrate by example how you would like those around you to be.

To help you with this, you can download a free Before I Go Conversation Starter Kit here: **www.beforeigosolutions.com/guidepdf.**

5

Grief and Bereavement

· · · · · ·

"Everything that has a beginning has an end.
Make your peace with that and all will be well."

— **BUDDHA**, Indian philosopher 624 – 543 B.C.

Generally speaking, grief is often also an elephant in the room in Western society. However, it is in fact the natural process in response to a loss of any kind, be it a death of a person, a pet, a way of life, divorce, a job; any kind of loss at all, whether big or little. In this section we are focusing only on bereavement, but please remember that what is said here can be applied to any situation where there is an ending.

Lessening the Taboo of Grief

In order to be more at ease with dying and death, we also need to be more at ease with grief, loss and bereavement itself. In Western society, it is often the case that bereaved people find themselves apologizing when they cry; being embarrassed when angry; or just feeling awkward full stop. This is partly because we as a society have become unfamiliar with dying and death, and therefore unfamiliar with grief. For instance, many men still think that it is not okay to cry, or to express emotion of any kind. John, a neighbour who was grieving the loss of his mother found himself simply unable to shed a tear. Even at the funeral, where he considered crying would be acceptable, he was full of emotion but unable to let it out. As time progressed, he found himself feeling guilty for not crying on top of everything else. Not helpful.

Another common belief is that it really is not acceptable to feel angry when someone has died. Yet many, many people find that anything from irritation to feeling beside themselves with fury is one of their responses to being bereaved. Sometimes this rage is turned into a positive action, such as raising money for a cause on behalf of the deceased person. When that happens, the rage has a chance to be channelled in a way that works. It's when it is judged to be 'wrong' that trouble happens, as, like all emotions that are suppressed, it has to come out in some way. That could be anything from unnecessary offensive remarks, to depression, to physical illnesses.

Many people think that grieving just takes time, and that after a while, the bereaved person will begin to feel better. Attached to these kinds of thoughts are a length of time which they think, or have learnt for themselves, is the appropriate time to grieve. A colleague told me about six months after my husband died that it would take at least two years before I began to feel like I was human again. He expressed this because that is what had happened for him, when his wife had died some years previously. For me to be told this at a time when every day was still an agony to get through wasn't helpful. Two years felt like a distant shore that was unbearably far away. It is really easy to underestimate how pervasive grief can be, and how long-lasting.

I know I was really shocked at how discombobulated I was after Philip died. Even though I had studied this topic professionally, even though I had read extensively about it, even though I understood in my mind what was happening – nothing had prepared me for the emotional onslaught of grief. Particularly in the first year of being bereaved, my emotions were all over the place. I knew anger, depression, regret, guilt, trying to bargain, fear, denial, and thinking I had accepted the situation were all normal things to be feeling, but I was unprepared for the topsy-turvy nature of this. A day could go by thus: 'Oh, no. No energy. Feeling very low. Not interested in anything or anyone. Just want to hide.' Then 'What? Has he died? How could that have happened?' And later, 'I'm so bloody angry with you, Philip! How could you let this happen? How *DARE* you die on me!' And then, tiny moments of acceptance before another emotion whooshed through, or denial visited again.

What Is Grief?

Grief therefore affects people in many ways, and the more we know about these ways, the better. With knowledge can come understanding, and with that can come compassion, acceptance and kindness, both for ourselves if we are grieving, and for our family members and friends.

How Grief Shows Up

If you are grieving yourself, give yourself plenty of time and go through the effects listed below, ticking off what ones you recognize you have felt. If you know someone who is grieving, identify which of these you think you have witnessed in that person, or what you think they may be feeling. If you don't know anyone who is grieving, read through them anyway to familiarize yourself with the effects of grief, so you can be more compassionate and understanding to others who are. Take it bit by bit – this can be intense reading.

Physical Effects of Grief:

- Utter exhaustion, muscle tightness or weakness, lack of energy
- Feeling restless all the time
- Headaches; tightness or heaviness in the throat
- Panic or anxiety attacks
- Loss of appetite – or mindless bingeing or eating of things you would not normally eat
- Digestive upsets; constant nausea
- Pain in parts of the body, including aching muscles and/or numbness
- Finding it hard to go to sleep; feeling fearful of sleeping; or waking up at odd times; disturbing dreams
- Difficulty concentrating – forgetfulness, absent-mindedness
- Difficulty making decisions
- Empty feeling in the centre of your body

"I never usually had headaches, but these would come on quite suddenly and would not respond to any amount of pain-killers. The only thing I could do was sit and watch mindless TV (I couldn't concentrate on anything more demanding) or read a light-hearted novel."

— Jean, Scotland

"The night I heard my boss was killed suddenly in a car accident, I had excruciating pain from my thighs down. In the morning it had gone."

— Serena, Australia

"Having been an early to bed person all my life, I found it impossible to sleep before 2 am for many months after my wife died."

— Stephen, England

Emotional Effects of Grief:

- Numbness - not feeling anything at all
- Shock and disbelief (even if the death was expected)
- Increased irritability, frustration or short-temperedness; impatience
- Detachment from the usual things in life that give you pleasure
- Bitterness and resentment (towards the person who has died, towards God, towards others)
- Relief - especially if you have been a caregiver for a long period of time
- Regret - about things unsaid, or said, or dreams not realized
- Guilt - about the above, or sometimes feelings of 'why them, why not me?'
- Anxiety, worry and fear
- Anger - you may be angry at your loved one for leaving you, angry at the situation that caused the death (e.g., a drunk driver), the doctors (for not being able to save them), God (for allowing it to happen), yourself (for not doing enough, or preventing it, or not taking action soon enough) or the whole world.
- Sadness and yearning - may or may not include tears
- Feeling embarrassed about your feelings
- Loneliness and/or yearning for your loved one
- Feeling worthless

"It all happened so fast. Even though we knew he was terminally ill, I didn't expect it to happen when it did."

— Kate, Canada

"I miss my wife's warm presence in our bed so much. I miss the cuddles."

— Michael, England

"Grief is a strange feeling inside. You go along happy and full of life, then something or someone will remind you of the person who died and all of a sudden everything stops, a flood of emotions wash over you, and you're reminded of being without them and the pain is so overwhelming."

— Laura, USA

Mental Effects of Grief:

- Inability to concentrate or finish tasks
- Forgetfulness
- Inability to make decisions, even about small things
- Forgetting where things go in the house - e.g., putting milk in the oven, a hot meal in the fridge
- Being a bit accident prone (tripping, bashing into furniture, feeling wobbly on your legs)
- Confusion

"I completely forgot today that I was going to meet my best friend. That's never happened before. I am all over the place."

— Penny, England

"After completing a session on our affairs for the lawyer, I walked straight into our sliding glass doors. Gave myself a huge black eye. That wouldn't have happened if I was okay."

— Peter, USA

Social Effects of Grief:

- Wanting to have people around you all the time, or none of the time
- Needing to hide yourself away
- Finding large groups of people impossible to be among
- Wanting only to talk to your loved one, and therefore not talking to anyone else
- Needing to tell the story over and over again, or speak constantly of your loved one
- Wanting to keep your grief entirely private
- Worrying you will be taking up too many people's time (and therefore not asking for help)
- Loss of some 'friends' and/or gaining of others
- Feeling lost and lonely; disconnected from others
- Having lots of spare time and not knowing what to do with it
- Needing hugs and physical contact, or pushing it away
- Feeling disinterested in any of your friends' day-to-day lives
- Disappointment with lack of support

"I was afraid I would be boring to my friends, when all I wanted to do was talk about Greg. So I pretended I was doing okay. Then I went home and bawled my eyes out."

— Heather, Scotland

"I coped by being around others at work and at home as much as I possibly could. The last thing I wanted to do was be on my own."

— John, USA

Psychological Effects of Grief:

- Overwhelming thoughts
- Suicidal thoughts
- Poor concentration
- Wishing one was not alive
- Avoidance of thinking about what has happened
- Inability to make decisions
- Numbness
- Shut down and thus not managing daily life very well

"I stopped wanting to live myself. I didn't actively want to kill myself or anything, but I lost all interest in carrying on. I did, of course, but it was just going through the motions."

— Alwyne, USA

Spiritual Effects of Grief:

- Wondering what is the point of life
- Difficulty in understanding how God (or your religion icon) could have allowed this
- Questioning your faith
- Loss of interest in your religion or faith - or an increased dependency
- Wondering about the meaning of life and death
- Doubting what you have always known and lived your life by
- Acceptance of the journey
- Belief in enlightenment
- Inability to see the point in continuing to live yourself

"I did wonder what on earth was the point of living after my daughter died. There just seemed no point in getting up in the morning, no point to anything at all."

— Helga, USA

"Everything I had believed in seemed to just go out the window. Like I had not only lost my husband and best friend, but my whole way of life, and all the beliefs I had too. It felt like another bereavement all over again."

— Marion, USA

Behavioural Effects of Grief:

- Risky behaviour such as drinking too heavily or driving too fast
- Loss of self-confidence
- Being a workaholic
- Withdrawal from family and friends: isolating oneself
- Forgetfulness
- Disinterested in the usual activities
- Lack of care for oneself
- Crying at odd times

"The effect of several family deaths in the space of two years left me terrified, and unable to do any of the things I usually did. I was shocked at how scared I became."

— Mhairi, Scotland

Other Effects of Grief:

- Missing them
- Seeing/hearing/sensing the dead person
- Talking to them as if they were alive
- Not remembering anything bad (or good) about them
- Being afraid you will forget them
- Being preoccupied with thoughts or memories of them
- Only being able to remember horrible memories (this will change)
- Wearing their clothes, carrying treasured belongings representing him or her
- Developing his or her mannerisms
- Not remembering what they looked or sounded like

"I used to think I saw Margaret in the street. I would feel so excited, and relieved, only to have those feelings dashed as I realized it was not, could not, be her."

— Saul, USA

"The first morning I woke up and couldn't remember clearly what Vic looked like was devastating."

— Sheila, Canada

"For a long time, I couldn't get rid of the memory of Alice's face wreaked with pain. It was awful and I felt like this obliterated all the lovely memories. That did change, but it took far longer than I would have imagined."

— Don, Scotland

So long as the grief is moving, changing and emotions are up and down and all over the place, the grieving person is probably doing okay. Although the intensity of the emotions may or may not increase, the gap between what is felt intensely will increase over time. Only if it seems that someone is stuck and not able to come to terms with the death, unable to integrate what has happened into the new kind of life they have been propelled into, is specialist help really needed. Resources for this are at the end of this book.

Coping with the Emotional Upheaval

When I was grieving, the one thing I knew to hold onto, in a sea of uncharted and very stormy waters, was the idea that I needed to let the feelings be there. Not pretend; not judge; not dismiss or belittle them. I just needed to have them, to let them be there. I experienced many of the feelings listed above, and often in the space of a day too. I quickly learned what I now call Front Door, Back Door Thinking.

When feelings that we don't want to have come knocking on our door, we usually don't want to feel them, and so we naturally lock and bolt all the doors and windows, pull down the blinds and draw the curtains. This all helps to make us feel safe, or so we think. The trouble is, the feelings lurk around outside, waiting to come in. So trying to push them away like this just doesn't work, as ultimately we become trapped in our own house. Eventually the feelings will apparently slip away, but if they haven't been able to enter the house through the front door, they will seep into the ground and arrive in the house insidiously, without anyone noticing.

This is when they take up residence in the body, and how they can begin to affect your state of health. Instead, even though it's counter-intuitive, it is much healthier (for you, and for those around you) to answer that front door when the feeling comes knocking. Open the door, fling wide the windows, and unlock and open the back door too. So then the feeling can enter, be felt (which allows it to express itself) and thus can easily leave again by the back door.

I gave myself permission to open the doors anytime the feeling knocked, and it didn't matter where that happened. So occasionally, I had to leave a gathering almost as soon as I had arrived. I have lost count of the number of public places (department stores, restaurants, public parks) in which I sobbed. I often had to pull the car over, stop in the middle of a phone call, or interrupt a conversation. Slowly, very slowly, I began to be more okay with feeling even the most excruciating of feelings. They didn't feel any less painful, but I did know they would eventually leave. Essentially, when I stopped trying to push the feelings away, they would come in the door, pass through the house, and out again more quickly than if I had tried to keep the door closed. Afterwards, I would sometimes feel washed out, or cleansed. Other times exhausted, or energized. I couldn't plan anything, because I had no idea how I would feel. Crying, which before used to make me feel better, didn't necessarily do this. But because of Front Door, Back Door Thinking, I trusted that the feelings would leave eventually, and I would be feeling a different emotion in the next short while. No wonder grief is known to be exhausting.

How Best to Be around People when They Are Grieving a Loss

One of the things I discovered when I was newly bereaved was how awkward people are when they meet you after they have first heard the news, and it can continue too, at other meetings. I quickly learnt it was often I who would be attempting to make them feel more at ease. This was okay with me; I wasn't really surprised as I had read about this happening. But it took energy, and was unnecessarily distressing.

CASE STORY: Loss of a Daughter

"I call grief living with the invisible disability, a disability that leaves you with no concentration span whatsoever. It leaves you a walking wisp of a zombie, it makes time slow down, and a task that took you two minutes will take you ten, if you are lucky. When I was in the fresh and early grips of grieving my four-month-old daughter, one of my only solaces was finally finding a dentist who was willing to take on the complexity of my very unique mouth. But I forgot my appointment twice. The first time I was charged, the second time they asked me to leave. It was a real kick when I was down, and due to the 'taboo-ness' of a society that doesn't talk about death, and particularly one that doesn't want to talk of something as 'unnatural' as a death of a child, I didn't feel like I could say to them what I really wanted to say, which was, 'I'm really sorry, I've just lost my daughter and my head is a bit all over the place, would you mind helping me remember my appointments somehow?'

Instead, I just quietly went away carrying the shame, embarrassment and the snap judgment of being labelled a time waster. I hope that we as a society can start to put something in place that recognizes that those living with grief are living with an invisible disability. We never know what another person is going through and it's hard not to make judgments, but if you are on the receiving end of one of those at the most vulnerable time in your life, it knocks you down with even more force, and takes you even longer to recover. Things you could brush off on a good day may take you months to recover from. It may sound silly, but I will never forget being kicked out of that dentist at that time, it scarred me for life."

– Tiffany Jane Crossara, Spain,
http://www.tiffanycrosara.com

Five Pointers to How to Be around Grieving People

1. **What Words to Use**
   Check in with whether you avoid using the word dead or death, and when. Perhaps it might be better to just say it as it is, as in, 'I was so sad to hear of X's death'. We will only get used to using these

words if we use them, so be a pioneer and let's include these words back into our vocabulary. I found that when people referred to Philip as having died, I would have one of two reactions. Either I'd be astonished that this had happened at all (hearing it out loud, out of someone else's mouth can bring it to life much more, pardon the pun) or I'd be glad they weren't pussy-footing around. Having said that, the word 'death' is a word that many have all sorts of thoughts and feelings around. They attach all manner of things, depending on their experience and circumstances. So using euphemisms can make it easier for people to hear what is being said. Tune into each situation and be sensitive.

2. **You Can't Get It Right**

   Once you recognize that nothing you can say or do can help much, and that you can't get it right, you'll experience more freedom to say whatever works for you. The sad fact with a death of a loved one is that other people cannot fix it. You can't fix it because it cannot be fixed. That person is never going to come back again in the way they were there when they were alive. It just isn't going to happen. So if you're someone who likes to fix things, then this could cause you some challenges. Watch out for those almost complacent sayings that are in fact designed to make the person delivering them feel better, rather than the bereaved person.

   "I think it's really lovely to recall something about the person who has died. So often people shy away from saying anything at all about that person, as if they're suddenly a taboo subject, when the bereaved person is really missing them. It's important to gauge whether they're ready to speak or not, so in the very early days, a simple comment such as 'I'll miss their sense of humour', or 'Their work will leave a great legacy', something complimentary but brief that requires no further conversation, is good. It leaves the bereaved open to talk if they want to and not if they don't. Later on, I think people want to speak about their deceased loved one but find that not many people are willing because they feel too awkward, so offering something like a cheerful anecdote is a great way to open conversation and let the bereaved person talk about them if they want to. Letting people remember, be sad and happy over the memories while in your company, is a great thing I think. You just need to be careful not to criticize the deceased or uncover something that might be controversial that the bereaved didn't know about."

— Katie, England

3. Acknowledge the Death

This is absolutely crucial, and you still might not get it right! If you don't live near the bereaved person, then your options to acknowledge the death are many and varied these days: text, messenger, email, phone, Skype, social media, sending a card through the post. No doubt there are and will be others too. But they have to be used wisely – many of these ways only work if they are the way you usually communicate with that person, and even then check in with yourself to see if it feels right. Listen to your tiniest instinct, and if you have even the smallest query about it, then don't do it. Communicate another way instead. Try to put yourself in their place; how would you like to receive the acknowledgment or condolences upon a death? I know I was very touched by the number of people who sent cards, which meant that often they had gone to the trouble of finding my address. I did also receive a lot of emails, but I haven't kept those in the same way that the cards have been kept, and looking at the cards was one way of feeling loved and less lonely at a harrowing time. If you find yourself tongue-tied, awkward and embarrassed about dying, death or grief, send a bereavement card with the words already written for you (see Resources Section).

4. Offering Help

Nearly always, people want to reach out and be helpful to a bereaved person. However, also they often simply let it be known that they are there to help, if anything is needed, as in, 'Let me know if there is anything I can do for you.' The problem with this, while it is nice to know, is that someone who is grieving is often not thinking straight enough to realize what they might need help with. This is because many of the normal, everyday things of life can seem quite irrelevant in the face of death. Even the basics such as eating, sleeping, or taking care of children. So it is much better to offer specifics. For instance, I work from home, and after Philip died it was so helpful to me when a friend rang and told me he went down to the Post Office every day, and would call by to collect something if I needed anything mailed. Another acquaintance turned up at the door one morning, saying they would like to cut the grass for me.

I felt hugely grateful to these people who were expressing their support for me in such a thoughtful and practical manner. So by all means cook food for a bereaved person (which is common), but there are many other things that can be done too. Even sitting with someone while they make phone calls to utility companies, or offering to do that for them, will likely be very much appreciated. When your head is all over the place, and the only thing you really want is for your loved one to be back, nothing else seems that important; so help with matters that do need to be attended to can be very useful.

5. **Be Patient**
   The length of time grief lasts can vary enormously, and is dependent on whether the death was expected or unexpected, the age of the person who died, the circumstances, the gender of the person grieving, whether there are past losses or not; all kinds of things. As a friend of someone who is grieving, you can support them best by keeping an eye out for aberrant behaviour in any way after the initial loss. Encourage them to get professional support, which can often be very helpful. Remember also that one doesn't 'get over' it. First of all, one never 'gets over' a bereavement. You just can't do that. It is not something one 'gets over' and then gets on with life. Rather it is something that becomes integrated into a new way of living, over time (see Resources).

You can get my free PDF download of *The 10 Best and Worst Things to Say to Someone Who Is Bereaved*. If nothing else, they provoke conversation as to whether you would use them or not! **www.beforeigosolutions.com /guide.pdf**

6

Ageing without Children

• • • • • •

*"When you've told someone that you've left them a legacy
the only decent thing to do is to die at once."*
— **SAMUEL BUTLER**, British novelist, 1835-1902

A common question in the *Before I Go* workshops and programmes is, 'What do I do if I have no children?' If this applies to you, whether you are childless, you have children but they live on the other side of the world, you are estranged from them, or they are no longer living, then you have an even more important responsibility to take care of your own end of life. It becomes really essential to consider whom amongst your friends, acquaintances or colleagues you would like to be an executor, power of attorney, and to organize your funeral. Who would you trust to carry out your end of life wishes, as per your advance directive? If you had been incapacitated in one way or another yesterday, what would happen to you? We tend to make an assumption that our family will carry out these duties for us, but it is different when we have no family available or none that are young enough.

This is an issue that, alongside the creeping realization that more and more people are getting older for longer and there are less and less resources to take care of them, has not yet been fully acknowledged. While the burden of elder care falls to families, what happens to those people who have no families?

In the USA, there are over 43 million family members providing some form of elder care for a person over 50 years of age. However, the 2010 US census stated that 11 million people over the age of 65 are living on their own, and this number is only going to increase.[7] Because family members provide most of the long-term caring support needed, what will happen to those who don't have children? In the UK, those over 65 without adult children are set to double from 1.2 million at the present time to 2 million by 2030. At the moment 92% of informal care is provided by family and 80% of older people with disabilities are cared for by either their spouse or adult children.[8] The older a person is, the more likely they are to be cared for by their adult child, and there are more older people now who need care than there are family members available to provide it.

> As the baby-boomer generation ages, a growing 'family care gap' will develop as the number of older people in need of care outstrips the number of adult children able to provide it. This is expected to occur for the first time in 2017.
> — The Generation Strain,
> Institute of Public Policy Research 2014

If you are someone who for whatever reason has no children or family members available to help care for you as you age, you need to research how best you can help yourself (see Resources). Here are some tips to help you do that:

1. **Take care of your insurance.** Investigate your particular insurance situation, in your country or state, and what it will and won't pay for. Knowing this information in advance will help you make informed and sensible decisions now.

2. **Complete your end of life plan.** This is just as important for you as to anyone with children; get it all done, bit by bit, starting now.

3. **Keep everything up to date.** Thus you can make sure your current wishes are honoured.

4. **Consider sharing a home.** Think about sharing with like-minded people, maybe some of them younger than you. This is becoming more and more common, as in pooling resources, getting together with friends and creating your own little family, or community. Co-housing units have been around for some time now – creating the kind of community that was the norm when we had more nuclear families.

5. **Widen your range of friends.** Make sure your friends are from different age groups, get involved with younger people and give to them some of what only you or your generation can give.

6. **Widen your interests**. Explore new things, meet new people, expand your mind and your horizons.

"I am single with no children and I think I will ask a new friend from a course I'm doing at the moment to be my power of attorney. We've got to know one another quite well and I think she'll be a good health and wellness power of attorney. Looking further ahead, I have a god-daughter who was married last year. In a few years' time when her life is a bit more settled I would think of asking her because she's younger."

— Penny, England

7

What Is a Body?

• • • • • •

"Eternity is now. Right now, right here, you're an infinite being.
Once you get past the fear of death as an end,
you merge with the infinite and feel the comfort and relief
that this realisation brings."

– **WAYNE DYER**, American philosopher, 1940-2015

In many Western countries, when you see a closed coffin at a funeral, it can be a shock. Imagining the person you loved in there is not always a pleasant picture. A lid over the top of a box in which a person lies is all wrong somehow, as it is when we draw a sheet over the face of a dead person – it is our way of saying, this is the end of their life. Never usually would a piece of material be drawn over someone's face. When you see a person's body wrapped in a shroud, this may be even more shocking. I remember the first time this happened to me, I turned up at the funeral and saw the body covered in a beautiful woollen embroidered shroud, and laid on a willow frame. I was a bit taken aback. It was so clearly a body shape, but with the head all covered up, as it needed to be. I was faced very much with the reality of the death of that person.

And yet, is it really true that they have died? Different religions say different things and have different beliefs about what happens to bodies; and then there are plenty who believe in anything from atheism to past lives to the existence of 'something else' that is unidentifiable.

My belief, and experience, is that if you recognize that what keeps you alive is something more than a body, then it may be much easier to complete the Taking Action section in this Guide. However, I didn't fully appreciate this until I watched my husband die, which I wrote about in *Gifted By Grief:*[9]

"Last night, 1st December 2011, dear Philip left his body at 8.19pm. I say left his body because it became very obvious that there was no longer an inhabitant in that body at that time. You may very well have seen this yourself – one moment the person is there, and the next moment, having taken their last breath, they are not. And that is death; that moment. Philip struggled in the last few days of being in the body. I have to say 'the' body instead of 'his' body, because it sounds too odd now to refer to him as having a body when it was so clear that the body was just the packaging for his spirit. Who Philip is was simply flowing through that form for that particular time."

A few days later, I referred to his body as an empty bag. In fact, about three weeks after he died, I woke up thinking, 'If that was an empty bag, then what is this?', (referring to my own body). It had been so definite: this inhabiting a body, and then not. Just like someone living in a house, and then moving out. The empty house has all the objects of the life that was lived there, but when the person no longer lives in the house, those objects are no longer useful. And so it seems with a body, although not everyone thinks like this by any means.

"Arriving two hours after my mother died, I walked into the hospital room and my first thought was, 'My goodness, she is SO beautiful!' I think this must have been the spirit of death I was viewing, because she had had a stroke and her mouth was all lopsided. Being there with her body has been one of the most beautiful experiences of my life."

— Joanna, Scotland

My belief is that when you can adjust your thinking to *having* a body, instead of *being* your body, then you can also begin to make a separation from identifying *with* your body. I know this might be confusing; it's not how we talk about it at all usually. Normally everyone is completely identified with their body. By that I mean we use language such as:

- I feel terrible
- I'm hungry
- I need some exercise

What we really mean when we say these things are: my body has an ache/pain/unspecified unwellness, my stomach is empty and wants to be filled up, and my body wants to stretch, run, walk, or be outside.

Notice that even in these examples I use the word 'my'. It's more true to say, 'this body that I inhabit'. More true maybe, but definitely clumsy! We all have shorthand that allows us to make more sense to each other, and avoid these kinds of truthful but clumsy phrases. The trouble is, we all believe this shorthand – we really believe that 'I' is my body and my hunger, ache or pain or need for exercise. Then we begin to take things personally when they don't go right for us, or according to the way we think they ought to go.

So I highly recommend beginning to dis-identify with your body by starting to create some distance from it, simply by acknowledging that you *have* a body, not that you *are* a body. As spiritual teacher Ramana Maharshi said: "Who am I? Not the body because it is decaying; not the mind, because the brain will decay with the body; not the personality nor the emotions, for these also will vanish with death." [10]

Who or What is 'I'?

This question, 'Who am I?' is a very useful one to ponder, if you are interested in reflecting on 'having' a body instead of 'being' one. It is used in many spiritual traditions, to help encourage people consider just what is meant by the idea of 'I'. Initially, when asking this question of oneself, we tend to answer 'a mother, daughter, sister; an accountant, co-worker, or artist'. These are actually roles we play, though, they are not who we are, even though we may identify with them. Notice as you dig deeper and deeper with this question what kind of thoughts pop up, and how you feel about it. Seek out some traditions that offer help in this kind of question (see Resource Section). You may well find that you begin to completely reconsider who you thought you were, and then it is not so far to the next step, where you can begin to observe your thoughts and examine them.

Many spiritual traditions also invite you to observe your thoughts, and indeed, many psychological traditions ask that too. So instead of being completely wrapped up in whatever the thoughts are, there is almost a separation that allows you to watch what thought is popping up, before your eyes, as it were. An example might be:

> "That's interesting. A thought that says, 'I want to have some chocolate now' is dancing in front of me. Hard to believe, as I am completely full with my dinner. But it is enticing me to believe it,

to take action and eat some chocolate. I'm going to wait and see if it is still there, tempting me, in 10 minutes or so."

When you can watch the thoughts do their dance for you, then it is easier to consider the idea that thinking itself is what determines whether we have a good time or a bad time, an enjoyable experience or not.

If you haven't come across this idea before (that our experience of our circumstances is not dependent on the circumstances themselves) then you may find it odd. Here's an example of when I first noticed this. I was in my late twenties, and travelling in India. The sun was hot, the sky blue, and I had wanted to do this for a long time. I was staying with a friend and exploring. I was not happy though; what I really wanted was to be with a man I was interested in, but he was en route to Bali, and I had no way of contacting him until after another few weeks had gone by (this was well before the internet and mobile phones).

I had sent a letter to the local Balinese Post Office where I thought he might be, and was waiting for a reply. Every day, I trekked to the Post Office in Calangute to see if there was a letter for me. As time went on and no letter arrived, my mood worsened. Nothing else had changed. I was still in an idyllic location with the sun constantly shining, and I was getting on well with my companion. I had made my happiness dependent on the receiving of a letter (and hopefully saying the words I wanted it to say!). I did realize this, and started using positive affirmations to try to change my mind. Although they worked for a bit, soon I would start feeling miserable, doubting and unhappy again. I was at the mercy of my thoughts.

It took many more years to understand that happiness is an inside job, that is, one can be happy regardless of the outside circumstances. It's all to do with how thought actually works. So while changing thoughts (as in affirmations) is a tool that can be useful sometimes, understanding that thought itself occurs and then is believed or not by who we really are, is very liberating. It means that you don't have to take any thoughts that appear to come from inside you that seriously – neither the ones you like, nor the ones you don't like.

The reason I'm introducing this idea here is because when you have the thought, 'I am a body' and you believe that to be true, it will dictate how you feel about that body, and it will likely be much more scary to contemplate the death of that body. When you notice a different thought being produced by your mind, such as, 'I have a body', then an obvious question arises, which is, 'Who is the I that has a body?' That ended up being one of the major gifts that Philip's death allowed me to access. When I saw his body lying there, just a few minutes after he had died, it was clear it was an empty bag. When a few weeks later I said to myself, 'What is this bag (my body) filled with? What is this 'I'? *Who* am I?' I embarked on a quest to find out, which is essentially what *Gifted By Grief* is all about.

Believing Your Thoughts

Is it possible that you could choose to not believe all your thoughts? What about if the thought you are thinking might just be a random thought, floating through the mind, like the, 'I want some chocolate' one, and not much to do with who you really are? I know that might sound wacky, but if you are intrigued by this I highly recommend checking out some of the books and other information on the Three Principles (see Resources, p. 174).

These are fundamental underlying principles of how the world really works; how the experience of our minds and bodies really works, and what we can do about situations now to completely change how we feel within them, without needing the actual situation to change. This is important, because most of the time, we focus on making outer changes in the hope that this will then affect our experience of our situation. So we say, 'I'm not very happy with my relationship at the moment. Somebody else might be much better for me.' Or 'I'm frustrated at work, what needs to happen in this department to lessen this frustration?' Or 'If only I had _____ then I would be happy.'

Even spiritual believers get caught up with this – it just takes a different form. So if you catch yourself attending workshop after workshop, or thinking 'I need to progress on the spiritual path before I can....' or 'If only I was more like that guru, then I'd be....' then you have fallen into the same trap, that of trying to change the outer rather than focusing on the inner. The human race has got the whole world back to front. Everything is upside down and the wrong way round, and that's one of the reasons why we find it so hard to face death; of ourselves, and of others.

When you are able to see that the body you inhabit is simply that – a temporary vehicle to allow the expression of who you really are, then it doesn't matter quite so much anymore when the body begins to die. (Having said that, it is all very well knowing you and your loved ones are not just a body, but it is still very painful indeed when someone you love is dying or has died.) However, if you think of the body as a complex machine, the running parts of which come to an end at some point, then it makes death much more bearable. For the death is then only of the machine, not of who you are. Instead, who you are is the stuff that inhabited that body, which never had a beginning, nor an end. It just exists. Just like all of life itself, which takes up forms of many different kinds temporarily. When the forms die, the essence continues, because it never began and never ends.

So when I looked at my friend's body wrapped in that beautiful shroud, I had to remind myself of exactly what I was looking at. It was the leftovers of who she had been. That was appropriate because the form gets left behind after life leaves, and has to be disposed of in a suitable way. Her essence (which is who she really is, was, and always will be) is still around, it just can't be seen in that form anymore. Some people will be able to sense it. Others will be the recipient of a visitation, dream or certain knowledge that she is still around. Some people have developed their sixth sense, the sense of intuitiveness and psychic ability, and are able to sense into this other dimension, although none of this discounts the sadness, sorrow and grief that arises when we lose someone whom we love.

Here's an experiment. Try creating some distance from your body by spending a day describing yourself in the third person. Use a very clumsy sentence such as 'This body named _____' instead of using the much more convenient word 'I'. Have fun with it. Watch what happens when you disassociate yourself from the body; notice your thoughts and feelings. Play around with how different it feels to say 'I'd love to go for a walk' and 'This body named _____ wants to go for a walk.' Or 'I'd love a cup of tea' and 'This body wants a cuppa.' Take it lightly and enjoy watching what happens.

Life and Death, Death and Life

When you begin to think about death, it's natural to also begin to contemplate the kind of life you are living. They go hand in hand. This can be seen really easily when someone has a near miss in an accident; or is diagnosed with a life-threatening illness; or knows someone who died or nearly died. We are stopped in our tracks and get to reflect on what is important to us now, while we are alive. This is one of the great gifts of death – it delivers an invitation to focus on what is happening right here, right now. Suddenly, life itself becomes very precious, in every way that it shows up, as quoted by Dennis Potter, a UK TV dramatist before he died in 1994, where he speaks of the paradox of being fully alive in the face of death:

"The blossom is out in full now, it's a plum tree, it looks like apple blossom but it's white. It's the whitest, frothiest blossomest blossom that ever could be, and I can see it. Things are both more trivial than they ever were and more important than they ever were, and the difference between the trivial and the important doesn't seem to matter. But the now-ness of everything is absolutely wondrous." [11]

Eckhart Tolle, author of *The Power of Now*, says: *"The secret to life is to die before you die – and find that there is no death."* It is indeed possible to include the paradox of life and death when you are willing to face up to, include, and even embrace the fact of your own death.

Thinking about the future and what you want to happen when you die could also be thought to be paradoxical – surely, when you are doing that you are not 'here now' as Potter said? But this kind of thinking is also done in the moment, right here, right now, as is everything you do. And so we are faced with one of the great paradoxes of life itself – it is only really experienced in the moment (that moment that has just passed). Everything else is imaginings in the form of thoughts, projecting into the future and wondering what will happen, or reflecting on the past and wishing it had been different (or appreciating it for what it was). Even these thoughts are happening in the moment, right now.

This is a huge topic. I am only touching on it briefly here. If you want to explore further, I recommend checking the Resources section and exploring with what tempts you there.

8

Attunement

● ● ● ● ● ●

"Life is not separate from death. It only looks that way."
— Blackfoot American Indian saying

I am an associate member of the famous Findhorn Foundation Community in the North of Scotland. The Community is a spiritual community, eco-village and learning establishment, with the Foundation itself at the core of what are currently about 500 members in one way or another. One of our traditions and identifying principles is attunement. This means we take time to focus within before the beginning of any day, project, task, period of work, or process where a decision has to be made. I want to invite you to do the same thing with the next section in this book. While the word itself often means to bring oneself and one's actions into harmony with another person, that is not the only meaning in our community. We also include being in a place of harmony within.

In practical terms, enabling this can be as simple as a deeper breath or two before you begin any task, conversation, meeting, or project. For instance, it is not unusual for meetings between people here to begin with a minute of silence. It is simply a time for those attending to perhaps close their eyes, reflect inwardly and take a pause from what has been going on before. It may be that you will check in with yourself, so to speak, as to where any anxiety, disturbance or unsettledness may be residing in your body. It might be that you simply use the time to let the cares of the day drop away. Or you might actively bring your mind to bear on the purpose of what you are about to do.

I want to invite you to attune before you read any of these following chapters, and especially before you answer any of the questions, take any of the actions or come to any decisions. It doesn't get any bigger than life and death and every section deserves your fullest and clearest attention. If when you are reading this section you aren't attracted towards attuning in this way, that's fine. The process of you getting your act together to read, ponder, question yourself and then answer the questions – and then write down your answers will work anyway! Attunement is not necessary for the completion of any section within this Guide. But if you are so inclined, it will bring another dimension to your thoughts and words that you may find more fully satisfying.

SECTION TWO

......

TAKING ACTION

Introduction

· · · · · ·

This section introduces you to actually creating your own end of life plan. Up until now we have been talking about it only; now comes the walking of the talk.

There are eight components to a good end of life plan: The Legals (including the will and power of attorney); Last Days Wishes (including advance directives); Household Arrangements (including financial affairs, decluttering and household organization); Funeral (including end of life celebration, costs and organization); Your Digital Life (all online information) and the Living Legacy (how you wish to be remembered), sharing it and writing it down.

The 8 Components of a Good End of Life Plan

Legals	Household	Digital Life	Shared
will, powers of attorney, finances and healthcare	includes financial affairs, organization, death cleaning	includes social media, photos, membership and all things online	all relevant people know about the plan and agree with it

Last Days	Funeral	Living Legacy	Written Down!
includes advance directives, anticipatory care documentation	includes memorial, and end of life celebration, other ritual endings	how you wish to be remembered and in what way	and easily locatable

Reasons to Complete Your End of Life Plan

- Makes everything very accessible, and easy to find, for your executor or anyone else taking care of your affairs, thus saving time and money.
- Helps your family and friends make decisions after you have died.
- Enables them to carry out what you wanted (which is very comforting to those grieving).
- Allows you to consider what is important to you and to make decisions about those things accordingly.
- Can help you come to terms with your own ending of life, even if you are not facing it right now.
- Can easily be updated as your circumstances change.
- Gives you and your family relief and peace of mind.
- Brings you a sense of being in control.
- Soothes the mind, which can worry and fret about 'what might happen'. Once it's all down in writing, there is no more worrying for the mind.

Getting Overwhelmed

It is very easy to get overwhelmed with the different areas of end of life matters and the many things to be considered in each section. This is partly because it is so difficult to project into the future and imagine our own death. Frankly, we avoid this whole topic generally so why would we want to imagine it happening at all, let alone in the future?

What makes this easier is if you say to yourself:

If I had died yesterday, what would I have wanted to happen?

Then the event is brought into the here and now. You will be able to much more easily imagine, given your existing life circumstances, what the answers might be. You can know right now, exactly what mess or muddle there would be – would your family be able to find this, would they be able to understand that? Would they not know what to do, or would they know exactly what to do? Asking this question is much better than asking, 'What if I die tomorrow?' You'll find the answers come more quickly when you contemplate the idea that today, you are no longer here, and given the state of your affairs right now, how that might impact your family and friends.

"Since your course, I now have a Death File, so does my husband; wills are up to date, the Advance Directive has been done and witnessed and is on its way to my doctor to be held with my records, and the workbook is completed and also sits in the Death File. My partner has done his side of things as well. It was a long, long road to do all this. It was difficult just from a practical point of view understanding what needed to be done. I got lost several times but kept on until it was done. I feel great to have done all this. It mattered, it really did, and I'm so glad I got prompted to do it."

— Jackie, Scotland

When you are creating your plan, it is very important to read the following and apply it:

Take Bite-sized Chunks

When you take a really dirty pan and are trying to scrub it clean, the water initially gets dirtier and darker. The soap suds disappear, the bits and bobs of leftover food float around, and there may be a greasy film on the water surface. In other words, it has to get worse before it gets better. That is quite often what it feels like when you are tending to end of life matters. So really hang in there because you *are* making a difference as you progress little bit by little bit. Keep on keeping on, and at some point you'll be able to see the equivalent of a really clean pan.

It's a Project!

Treat your end of life plan as a project, make a decision about how you'll get this done, and then commit to it. One very effective way to support yourself in this is creating a What I Did List. This is different from a 'to-do' or 'to be done list'. What goes on your What I Did List is everything you did in that day, whether or not it has anything to do with your end of life plan. It includes things like made breakfast, ate breakfast, washed up breakfast; you can put all that stuff on the list too, because it's amazing how much time that sort of thing takes up. At the end of the day you get to look back and impress yourself with how much you actually did do, and how you really spent your time. If within that you have a 10-minute chunk where you did something towards completing your plan, then that is brilliant and you can pat yourself on the back. It's a really good way of feeling great at the end of the day.

CASE STORY: Adriana

Adriana was a self-employed friend and work colleague, and one of our community, who had attended the second of my *Before I Go* workshops. She was not very well at the time, and her health continued to decline with a mysterious illness, despite her being only in her early sixties. Living alone, somewhat estranged from her family, she appreciated the importance of sorting out her affairs generally, and had documented in her plan very specific instructions on what she wanted, where everything was, and what was important to her, including writing a will.

One morning I heard she had been found dead in her apartment. This was a terrible shock, made worse by the fact that the police treated it as suspicious, and locked her apartment along with the plan in it. Fortunately, her executor knew she had been appointed, but nothing was able to be sorted out until access to the apartment was granted, which took several weeks. The police had also taken her computer. It was only after her body was released (despite cause of death still being unknown) that the keys to her apartment were returned and her close friend Pat could read Adriana's plan and discover what she wanted to have happen after her death. She was also able to get access to her computer, albeit with difficulty as the main password for it had not been written down. However, Adriana had given very clear instructions about her funeral, and to the best of their abilities, Pat and other close friends created a beautiful send-off for her.

There's three points in this case story that are important: first, when you complete your end of life plan you need to make it clear that if your loved ones cannot, for whatever reason, address your wishes as you have laid out, then that is okay with you. This really takes the pressure off those organizing your funeral, because it is a lot of work. Secondly, remember to include the most obvious passwords: those of your phone and your computer. Without these, it makes it much more difficult for people to access your files. Thirdly, make sure at least one person has a copy of your plan – if only this had happened in Adriana's case, then the organizational work for her funeral would have been made much easier. No-one would have been in limbo, and what was put together in just a matter of days could have been made much easier with more time.

9

Looking after the Legals and Financials

· · · · · ·

"A man who lives fully is prepared to die at any time."
— **MARK TWAIN**, American writer, 1835-1910

This chapter is based on an overview of all legalities and while giving some specifics as regards the laws in some countries, must be read as a general viewpoint only, and not necessarily applying to your case. You *must* make sure you research the laws in your country, state or jurisdiction, take professional advice, and act accordingly. However, there are similarities in all countries and that is what this chapter addresses.

ATTUNEMENT: Take a pause. After reading this paragraph, just close your eyes and notice your breathing, and how your body feels. Give yourself a moment or two, before reflecting on your thoughts about your legal and financial issues.

Wills

In the UK, almost 60% of people do not have a written will, [12] and the statistics are similar in the USA. This is unfortunate as having a will is a major part of your end of life plan. If you're like me, just the mention of the word 'will' is enough to cause your eyes to droop, your mind to wander, and to suddenly feel very attracted to washing up the dishes. Watch out! This is just your ego wanting to be in charge, and trying to determine what you should or shouldn't do. Instead, notice what is happening, just say hallo to the thought of washing up instead of engaging with it (or worse, actually doing it!) and then continue reading this section. Remember, you may want to attune first.

What Is a Will?

A will is a legal declaration by which a person (the testator) names one or more people to manage his or her estate, and provides for the distribution of his or her assets after death. 'Estate' is defined as finances, property, possessions of monetary value, and intellectual property such as music, books or digital documents.

What Is Probate?

If there is a will after someone has died, the executor or administrator will apply for a Grant of Probate. This grant is a legal document which confirms that the executor has the authority to deal with the deceased person's assets (property, money and belongings, known as their 'estate'). This process is called 'administering the estate'. In most countries, this process is similar, although in Scotland the process is known as 'confirmation'. In the USA, the laws in each state vary, so you must ensure you consult an attorney or other advice service to discover whether probate is necessary, or what is needed.

Why It's Important to Have a Will

Put simply, it will save your family and/or friends a lot of unnecessary time, money and hassle if you have one in place, even if your affairs are simple and you think you don't need to have one. There are many organizations in all countries that provide help with producing a will, and it's not in the remit of this book to go into this in detail. However, I can't stress how important it is to get it done. You will find charities all over the world who offer a free will writing service in the hope you will give them a donation in your will. The exact way this is done may vary from charity to charity, but if you have a favourite charity it is worthwhile asking if they offer a will service.

Visiting a Lawyer

Often the very thought of visiting a lawyer, attorney or solicitor can make one's heart drop. People have all kinds of ideas about them, not helped by the use of sometimes archaic, and often difficult to understand, language, that is used in the legal profession. However, they are just people. Treat them as you would when engaging a tradesman – shop around and find the best person for you and your circumstances. Make sure you like them, and also the firm they work for, as that particular person may not always be there. It is also good to remember that lawyers are not any better than you; not any more intelligent necessarily; and not more valuable to society than you – they just know more than you about a specialized subject. This is why you must feel at ease with the person you meet; you are going to be trusting them and the whole process.

Before You Visit a Lawyer

- **Make a list of all your assets.** The financial affairs section of your plan will help considerably with this.

- **Understand how your assets are owned.** This is different in different countries, so make sure you have researched as much as you can. If you have a joint bank account, for instance, the other signatory (-ies) on that will automatically receive all that is in that account after you have died. If you own property jointly, or think you do, this is more complex, so you need to get advice.

- **Don't assume you know who will inherit.** If you are not married or in a civil partnership, then your surviving partner does not necessarily have an automatic right to inherit. In many countries, this is not the case, regardless of how long you have been living together. Also, don't make assumptions about to whom your assets would pass if you don't have a will. For example, in New York, if you don't have a will and have a spouse and children, then (at the time of writing) your spouse will get the first $50,000 plus half the balance of your estate, while the children will get the other half. In England and Wales, the surviving spouse will keep all the assets up to £250,000, and all the personal possessions regardless of value. The remainder of the estate is then divided into halves with the spouse receiving one half, and the rest being divided equally between the surviving children. Make sure you are aware of the legal situation in your country or state, and that you keep up to date with any changes in the laws.

A lot of this research can be done by yourself online, and you then will visit a lawyer well-prepared and from a position of power. Too often, we look up to those in these roles of authority, which means it is easy to hand our power over to them, never a good idea. Some participants on my courses were so concerned about making an appointment with a legal organization, that I put together a PDF of questions to help them get what they needed. You can get a copy of *13 End of Life Plan Questions to Ask Your Lawyer* here: **www.beforeigosolutions.com/guidePDF**

Do your homework first, and then read the questions in the PDF, add your own and visit a lawyer properly prepared.

Surprises

One of the most challenging things you can do in a will is to leave a surprise. Let your family know your intentions – discuss these with them, involve them and ask for their thoughts. You want your will to be an administrative process, not an emotional upheaval, which will be happening anyway simply as a result of you having died. Your family definitely will not need a surprise at this time. Even a pleasant surprise can leave them thinking they wished they had been able to speak to you about it, or to thank you. At the very least, if you want to write something into your will that will be unexpected, then also leave a letter, to be kept with the will, explaining the thinking behind it. This will go a long way to helping your relatives and/or friends understand your motives.

Inheritance Tax

Keep up to date with what the tax inheritance threshold is for you in your country. If you think your estate will be subject to these laws, take advice, and definitely appoint a lawyer to prepare your will for you. Don't even begin to think you can do it without this professional assistance.

Dealings with Other Countries

If you have any dealings with any other country, whether having lived there, owning property there, or any other connection or query about another country, you must get legal advice. This is really important, and worth the expense. Be very careful not to inadvertently revoke a will in one jurisdiction when signing a will in another jurisdiction, and be aware that you may not know about what you don't know. So get advice, and always provide copies of other wills to your advisers. I heard of a man who was originally from another country but had been residing in the UK for over 20 years at the time of his death. He had drawn up a will himself, had appointed an executor and thought all was fine. On the surface that was true, until the authorities in his country of birth would not accept a will that had not been drawn up by a lawyer. This meant a further drawing out of the process, plus some of his assets went to family members whom he had not wanted to benefit.

Can I Make My Own Will?

If you think you can do your own will, because your affairs are very simple, you can download a template for your situation and for most countries online. In the UK, you can also purchase a paper will pack from stationers WH Smith. Make 100% sure any document you download is for your country and from a reputable source. If you do decide not to have a formal will but to write your own, this would only be legally enforceable if you have made it clear that it is a testamentary writing. This means by writing things such as 'After my death, I would like my sister to have my diamond ring' - i.e., a statement of testamentary intent. It also needs to be signed by you at the end. However, it is also much better, and clearer, if it is dated, signed on every page, witnessed, appoints executors, and deals with your whole estate.

Having said this, I highly recommend having your will drawn up by a lawyer. The risk you take with not having a solicitor or lawyer draw up even a simple will is a partial intestacy, that is, some but not all of your estate is effectively bequeathed. With a homemade will, there may be questions or scenarios that you haven't covered, simply because you didn't know that there was a question to ask in the first place.

If you are doing your own, make sure it is dated and witnessed by someone entirely different from any of the beneficiaries or their spouses, otherwise any bequest to them may be null and void. The will must also be witnessed in the proper manner otherwise the whole will may be at risk of being invalid. In some countries or states the will must also be notarized (see later section).

> "My will needs to be updated just because my ideas of what I want to have done have changed. I have an attachment to it that I can change easily."
>
> — Neena, England

Couples

If you're in a partnership or marriage with someone then think about your wills separately, and also think about them together. It's as if there are three entities – you, them, and the other entity which is your marriage, civil partnership or other arrangements. Depending on the complexities of your particular situation, this will either be easy and straightforward (i.e., you want to leave everything to each other), but if you have children together or separately, it becomes much more complex. Plus if you happen to die at the same time, this needs to be provided for. This makes the end of life conversation a big one which deserves quality time and attention, and professional input.

"I heard about making a joint will, which sounded sensible. When I investigated, I discovered that if I died, this will would of course still be valid for my husband. But if he then married someone else, the will would still be valid. So we decided to create separate wills, and have now done so."

— Joy, England

"We are needing to up-date our wills and get the practical things much more in order so that when one of us dies the other one isn't left with a whole load of work to do because our affairs aren't in order or easy to find. This is even more of an issue for people now that we do so much domestic stuff online (e.g., what do we do about our passwords?). And heaven forbid if Russell and I died at the same time. We all think it's a good idea to face up to what happens when we die, but it's truly difficult to make it a priority (unless of course you know you are going to die very soon – like next week). There really is a lot to think about and before working with *Before I Go Solutions*® I was so overwhelmed by the thought of it all that I didn't do anything (except hang on to an out of date will). What I'm finding now is that it's only because we have a fixed time to do homework that we get anything done at all – but thank goodness for that!"

— Delcia and Russell, England

Appointing an Executor(s)

The executor is the person named in your will who will deal with your finances and possessions after you have died. In most countries you are allowed to have more than one executor but there may be a maximum to how many you can have. For example, at the time of writing, in Scotland, any number are allowed but in England and Wales, a maximum of four is allowed. However, it is advisable to appoint at least two people, either jointly or with one as a substitute, just in case a person named as a sole executor dies before you, at which point you may not remember to update your will, or you may not have the capacity to do so.

Who Should an Executor Be?

The executor can be anyone at all; it doesn't need to be a lawyer. However, it is important to think through who would be the most sensible choice for an executor in your particular circumstances. For instance, you might choose one of your children (the one best suited to the job, as there is quite a lot involved in carrying out the duties of an executor, see below). If you have a blended family as a result of second marriages, you might choose a lawyer for your executor as they will be less emotionally involved, though of course they will charge for their services.

Ask yourself – would _____ be able to deal with my estate by themself? If you have no family, you will either need to appoint a lawyer or ask a close friend. Make sure they know what it entails first, and usually a generation below you is a good idea, or at least a decade younger, as they are more likely to live longer than you.

> "I have the great good fortune of belonging to a women's accountability circle – five women that have been meeting for ten years, monthly, to challenge each other. We know each other very well. One of them is my executor. If she's gone, it will go to another one, so I have four choices, and they're all younger than me. I would put my future in their hands, easily, because, I know that they know me well enough, to know what I would choose."
>
> — Margaret, USA

What an Executor Has to Do

The responsibility of an executor is to identify the assets of the estate and assess their value at the date of death; identify the deceased's debts and pay them; and distribute the estate. There are many duties which an executor has to carry out in these three areas, and in most countries when a family member dies, you will be given information about what to do next. As an introduction, and to help you decide whom you wish to appoint as your executor, some of their duties are listed below. Each section includes several administrative tasks, so choose your executor(s) carefully.

1. **Legal**
   - Identify whether or not probate is needed.
   - If so, apply for a grant of probate to prove to those institutions and authorities that hold assets in the name of the person who has died that the executors have the authority to deal with the estate.
   - Identify and deal with any claims against the estate.

2. **Administration**
   - Take an inventory of the deceased's possessions and debts.
   - Notify and correspond with all relevant organizations so you can list all the assets.
   - Pay all bills and any other charges on the estate, including any debts.
   - Search for any unclaimed or missing assets.
   - Distribute the legacies.
   - Prepare and distribute estate accounts if necessary.
   - Distribute the residue of the estate to the beneficiaries.
   - Follow the wishes of the person who wrote the will (the testator) as closely as possible.

3. **Tax**
   - Complete inheritance tax returns and pay any inheritance tax due.
   - Complete any income and capital gains tax returns and pay any outstanding tax.

If you would like your executor to be paid for carrying out the above, this can be stipulated in your will, and can be conditional on them doing the job. If your executor is a lawyer, they will of course charge you, along with any other costs they incur. You may also want to think about whether your executor would be capable of administering any online presence you have. It may be worthwhile asking a separate person to do this. (See section on Digital Presence, page 159).

Notarization

Notarization is the official fraud-deterrent process that assures the parties of a transaction that a document is authentic, and can be trusted. It is a three-part process, performed by a Notary Public, that includes vetting, certifying and record-keeping. There are different rules in different countries for notarizing, so please check this out in relation to the country where you live.

Guardianship

A guardian is someone you have named in your will as the person you would like to be responsible for your children if they are orphaned before reaching the age of 18. This is an unbearable situation to think about, of course, but you must appoint guardians in your will if you have minor children. Otherwise, you risk the courts appointing someone to bring them up whom you would not have chosen. By appointing guardians, and naming them in your will, you will ensure that your children are looked after by those you consider best able to do so. As with most clauses in your will, you can include your first choice guardians and also a back-up plan. Again, in different countries this may be legally enforceable or not. For instance, in Scotland, appointing a guardian for your children in your will is simply an expression of your wishes and is not legally enforceable. In the event of any doubt or dispute about who the guardian should be, a Sheriff would make the final decision as to what was in the children's best interests, but again, it is much better to have it written down anyway.

"Last week I completed and notarized my will, and within this I set the person I wanted as guardian of my child. This feels like a great accomplishment. Wouldn't have done it without this group!"
— Myste, Canada

Blended Families

If you are part of a family that has blended together (i.e., you both have children from a previous marriage or partnership, and/or children together) then you have even more of a responsibility to make sure you have a will that is kept up to date, and reflects your wishes. This will mean a conversation with your partner, at the very least, and can be an area fraught with difficulties, especially where money is concerned. You may find it helpful to identify what each of you would ideally like separately, and then come together to see where you cross over, where not, and how you can come to an agreement that works for you both, and all the children and grandchildren involved. This is definitely an area where you will need specialist help.

"When we did our will we had to account for who all the children are, and how we wanted to divide stuff up, but since we don't have much in the way of money we have attached an inventory; it's an attachment to the will. It's mentioned in the will but it's separate so we can keep changing it as we go along."
— Diane, Canada

"This class has gotten me in conversation with my son's dad about updating our own plans for our son now that he is 15 and in a whole different situation than when we first wrote our will and he was a baby!"

— Sherry, USA

Estranged Children

Estranged children or children with whom you simply have no contact, and indeed might never have contact with, need to be thought about, depending on the laws in your country. In Scotland, regardless of the circumstances, every child has a right to claim part of their parents' estates, unless they have been formally adopted by someone else. A local lawyer told me that quite a lot of people are really dismayed to find out that they can't completely disinherit a child by simply not mentioning him or her in their will. She spoke of one man who had had a child as the result of a one-night stand. He had never had any relationship with this child, nor had he told his now-wife and their children that he had had another child. After a death, legally *all* children have to be informed of their rights in their parent's estate, and it can be very awkward indeed, for all concerned, if a surprise child suddenly pops up. So make sure you know the situation for your jurisdiction.

Keeping the Will Updated

There is little point in having a will if it doesn't express your wishes. However, these are likely to change over the course of your life, and so it's important to keep your will updated. Otherwise, when you die, the distribution of your estate will be determined by whatever is in your last valid will. A good time to review your will is each year on your birthday – it is amazing how easy it is to forget what you have written. Put it down in your diary and then just do it when the time comes. It will take you a few minutes to review, if that, and you may not need to make any changes. A few minutes for peace of mind for a whole year; not bad!

When updating the will (see final chapter on keeping your whole end of life plan updated), you either need to prepare and get signed a new will, which revokes the old one, or attach what is known as a codicil to the existing will. Any other way of amending your will is likely to make it invalid, so if you need to make a change, legal advice may be appropriate. Despite it often being thought that if you don't make a will, everything you leave will go to the state, this only actually happens in extreme cases, and after much investigation into the existence and whereabouts of relatives. However, it also takes a lot of time and money, so it is still better to have a will.

Trusts and Trusting

This book does not go into the ins and outs of trust funds. However, using wills and trusts together, or separately, can help you to protect your assets. The trust acts like a safety deposit box for your assets. You fund the trust with your assets while living and thus when you die, instead of the estate going to probate, it is afforded the protection of the trust. There are various pros and cons to both, for example, the tax implications for a trust may be less than those associated with a will. However, many of the considerations when creating a will would also apply to trusts. The laws about trusts are different in different countries, so speak to a local lawyer to discover the best requirements for your situation.

If you want your wishes to be obeyed, no matter what, then they need to be in a legal document, whether it is a will, a trust or a combination. If you don't want to go this far, but still want to have your wishes respected, you can maximize your chances of this happening by noting them down in your plan. You need to be fully aware that this is not a legal document, and therefore you will be 100% trusting that whoever receives it will carry out your wishes. Clearly, there will be some things you want to be legally binding (these go in your will) and others that don't matter so much (those go in the plan).

The other kind of trust is definitely worth a mention here. You trust that whoever receives your plan will carry out your instructions as listed within it. As you are not going to be around, you may think right now that you don't care whether they actually do this or not. However, not to labour a point, when you are dead you will not be able to do anything about it, so take some time to think about it! Pause right now, as you are reading this, and take a few moments to attune to how important it is that your wishes get attended to. The answer that comes will determine what you will do with your will and in your plan.

Let's say it again: unless you have what you care about written down in a valid, legal document such as a will, you don't know if the person you 'trust' is actually going to carry out what you have stated in your plan. So it is worth really paying attention to this issue of who you trust, and how that will affect your actions.

In the Advance Directive section, I write about the importance of giving a context for people, so they know why you have made the decisions you have made, and what were the reasons behind them. This applies to wills too; if you wish, you can state (either in the will, or out of it) why you are leaving £5,000 to James, and £10,000 to Mary. You can state your thinking regarding wanting your brother's daughter to have a certain piece of jewellery, and, e.g., your sister's daughter a valuable painting. It really helps the beneficiaries if they understand your motives. If you are not making any provision for a person for whom you may be expected to provide, in England and Wales you can discuss with your professional adviser the drawing up of a letter of wishes. If a challenge is made to your will, a judge is obliged to consider, amongst other things, whether you forgot to provide for your former spouse or estranged child or other dependant person. Thus the more background information you can provide, the better.

Copyright and Intellectual Property

If intellectual property is part of your estate, then you need to research the local laws regarding this. Stating what your successors can and cannot do with your IP, and preparing in advance for shared ownership and determining who those people may be, will be very important, depending on the importance of the IP to you. For instance, in the UK and USA, copyright protection of music and literary works expires 70 years after the author's death. In the UK, for sound recordings, copyright expires 50 years from the end of the calendar year in which the recording is made. If, during that period, the recording is published or played/communicated in public, copyright will expire 70 years from the end of the calendar year in which it was first published or played/communicated. So you see how the importance of this depends on how important to you your intellectual property is.

> "What I do with my written property is to mail a copy of it to myself, signed across the tape, to lock in the date I owned it. Then I keep the package without opening it for future proof."
> — Dee, Canada

Power of Attorney

This is a general introduction and to be referred to as such. Research your own country or state as to what applies in your particular situation.

What Is a Power of Attorney?

The power of attorney is a legal document that states the name of the person or people ('attorneys') who is or are appointed to take action on your behalf if you are incapacitated. This may be incapacitated healthwise in any way, and unable to represent yourself, but also from a financial point of view if you are unable to run your finances for any reason. You may have different people for each one, or the same person or people for both. One attorney only means that if they die, then you no longer have someone to represent you, so having more than one is sensible.

A power of attorney is named in slightly different ways in different countries, however they are referring to the same kind of documentation. For instance, in Scotland a financial power of attorney is also called a continuing power of attorney. In England and Wales it is known as a lasting power of attorney. In California, a power of attorney may be general or specific.

> "Think of POA's like you think of insurance – you hope you will never need to use it, but if you do, it will be very handy!"
> — Cynthia, England

Health or Welfare POA

This comes into effect when the person is incapacitated in some way, whether physically or mentally. Different countries have their own laws on what incapacitated means. For example, in Scotland the law generally presumes that adults i.e., those over the age of 16, are capable of making personal decisions for themselves and of managing their own affairs. The starting point is a presumption that they are capable and this can only be overturned where there is medical evidence stating otherwise. Thus 'incapable' means incapable of acting; making, communicating or understanding decisions; or retaining the memory of decisions.

Deciding whether or not someone has capacity is also very task specific, for instance, can the adult make a decision about whether he/she wants coffee or tea, where to live, or manage a very simple bank account? Interestingly, the final decision about whether or not someone has capacity is a legal one, not a medical one. Again, this will be different in different countries, but the points made here raise questions you may not previously have thought of. So you can see that having a welfare POA in place in advance is a form of insurance – none of this may happen to you, and you of course hope that it won't, but in case it does, the legal documentation is in place to enable someone whom you trust (your named welfare POA) to act and make decisions on your behalf.

A Financial POA

This gives power to the appointed person to administer your financial and property affairs. The power may start immediately on registration of the POA, and will continue in the event of your incapacity or it may begin at a later date e.g., if you become incapable. It is your choice when the power of attorney is to begin; when you die, it ends.

Who Should I Appoint as My POA?

Generally speaking, it is a good idea to have someone a bit younger than you to be your power of attorney, simply because they're more likely to live longer than you. It doesn't have to be a family member; it could be a friend. They will be the person legally responsible for making decisions on your behalf, that is financial ones, and/or health-based ones. However, it is often the case that if you are in a partnership, this is the person who knows you best and whom you would choose, in which case you should think about appointing another, younger, person as well.

> "I've asked my stepbrother's wife to be my health and welfare POA. She's about twenty years younger than me and is really interested in health. She used to be a care-giver, and I think she would be great, very capable."
>
> — Albert, USA

How Many Can I have?

This is different in different countries and states. For example, in England and Wales you can appoint more than one, and they can be appointed so they can act jointly or severally (meaning separately). If you have more than one, then it means that you still have a valid POA if one of them dies, which is always handy. If you appoint them jointly, then they all need to agree on any decision, and the document may end on the death of any attorney; if you appoint them separately then one POA can make decisions on their own *or* with the other attorneys. Alternatively, you could give instructions for some decisions to be made jointly and others severally. Make sure you check what applies in your jurisdiction.

"When Armen needed non-emergency surgery, his son Michael (who has power of attorney for Armen's healthcare, and finances) had to sign the consent form. Armen had previously appointed 3POA names, but both the primary name and one of the secondary names had died. However, Armen had had the secondary names (Diane and Michael) specified as co-POAs.

This meant Michael had to show Diane's death certificate each time a signature was required, to prove she was dead and therefore couldn't co-sign. Of course this was a nightmare, and Armen couldn't change it because he was already deemed legally incompetent to sign a legal document. His son was finally able to get it changed, by using a Notary Public, since he had legal POA. He also used a Notary to add me to the HealthCare POA, so I can also make healthcare decisions and sign consents etc., on behalf of Armen. What I got out of this is not to name people as joint or co-signers or decision-makers – it makes it so much more complicated. And also have several alternatives to the primary person, if possible, as you never know who is going to die first!"

— Barbara, California

What to Do If You Can't Think of Anyone to Be Your POA?

This can be a challenge if you have no family, are estranged from them, or they live very far away. In the latter case, even if they live on the other side of the world you can still have them be your POA, but it will be made much more difficult because of the distance. Hence I would highly recommend having someone closer by. This could be a friend, neighbour, a colleague, your accountant, a lawyer or other professional. It could be someone from your church or spiritual group; a financial advisor or anyone whom you feel comfortable with taking decisions on your behalf, about your finances and about your health. If you do appoint someone who lives at a distance, think about naming a local contact who knows you well, with whom your POA can liaise.

Consider what you know about how their values match your own. Invite them out to tea and ask them about their own arrangements. Do some research. You'll get more ideas and perhaps someone you can trust who will volunteer to help you, or you may find you can be each other's POA's. Even though this is a serious subject, take it lightly and trust that the right person will come along, if you hold in the back of your mind the intention to find someone who is suitable. Be clear about your values and the kind of values you would like that person to have, take action when you can, and then see what opportunities life brings you.

> "Success! My new accountant has confirmed that she is willing to act as my Financial Attorney, should the need arise (and of course, hopefully it won't!). Phew – I'm amazed at how relieved I feel...."
>
> — Christina, England

Now you're at the end of this section, I invite you to attune once more. This helps, particularly when you are dealing with the intensity of legal, official or challenging matters such as the kinds of documentation in this section.

Just close your eyes, breathe deeply three times, and bring your attention to how that feels inside your nostrils, as cool air is taken in, and warmer air breathed out.

Check in with how the rest of your body is feeling. What word would you use to describe that feeling? If you decide to have a break, fine; but make a point of noting when you will return to continue creating your end of life plan, or which part of this Guide you will dip into next.

Advance Directives

This is known by several different names (Advance Decision, Advance Health Care Directive, Advance Directive, Living Will). For ease I will use the term AD to cover them all. They all mean the same kind of document – a statement which outlines what treatment you wish or wish not to have towards the end of your life, should you be unable to communicate for yourself. In some countries or states it is a legal document; you need to check what the legal requirements are for where you live. For instance, at the time of writing, an Advance Directive in Scotland is not legally binding. However, if there is one in place, the medical team will respect it and do what they can to follow the instructions laid out.

Advance Statements

These are more informal documents outlining the reasoning behind the decisions made in your AD. This is particularly useful for those who need to carry out your decisions on your behalf – when the background is understood to the decision making, it is much easier for them to make sure your wishes are complied with.

> "It's good to be clear, and state very clearly what you would like, but it's also worth giving some sort of reason as to why you made your decisions, because then that helps people understand the context in which you are doing it."
>
> — Richard, England

Why Do an Advance Directive and Statement?

While it's hard enough to face up to the fact that you are going to die one day, contemplating the means by which that might happen can be very off-putting. The fact of the matter though, is that those people who do have the courage to record their wishes, and keep them up to date, are more likely to die well. Statistics from Compassion in Dying [13] showed that 52% of those whose end of life wishes had been formally recorded were reported as dying in a good way, whereas, for those whose wishes weren't recorded, only 37% died in a good way.

In the UK, only 4% have completed AD's - lots of room for improvement here. In the USA, this figure is higher (about 30%), but essentially, if you care about the kind of treatment you may or may not receive at the end of your own life, and want to maximize your chances of receiving that, then planning ahead and creating an AD is essential, no matter where you live.

> "A lot of this depends on this thing of quality of life, and I don't want to be kept going if there's no quality of life to enjoy. I have seen a lot of care of the elderly in my career where the people being cared for basically are there, they are alive, but life is so dreadful, boring, and pointless. I really wouldn't want that myself."
>
> — Richard, England

We cannot, of course, know what will actually happen when we die, or how exactly it will occur. We cannot predict the timing, the nature, or the run up to it, although we can of course make some generalities, and do all we can to minimize the risks of dying early (as in healthy living) and maximize the ease of dying (as with AD's). After all this though, it is still a 'fingers crossed' job. To be certain of how you will die is not in the remit of this book, as in voluntary euthanasia, suicide or assisted dying. However, to create an end of life plan clearly helps to soothe the mind while we are alive, to help relatives after we have gone, and bring relief to all concerned, both before and after death.

What Does a 'Good Death' Mean?

Usually we think dying well (or a good death) to mean no pain or suffering, and surrounded by loved ones. If dying has to happen at all, peacefully is the word that most people want associated with it. To help you get clearer about what dying well means to you, here's some more specific questions for you to answer:

- Do you want to live as long as possible, no matter what?
- When you consider nearing the end of your life, do you feel the quality of the time you have left is more important than quantity?
- If you knew you'd had a stroke, and your ability to move and speak would be compromised, would you want to receive treatment if you contracted an infection?
- Imagine you've had a heart attack right now, would you want to be resuscitated?
- If you knew you had a terminal illness, would you want to receive antibiotics if you contracted pneumonia?

These are the kinds of questions you need to think about, and which are discussed in the *Before I Go Solutions* ® courses, or about which you can have a conversation with your family and friends. This is important, because you never know what will actually happen.

> "Both myself and my partner have AD's. He has serious heart problems and was again rushed into hospital last Tuesday. We were told that they didn't think they could do anything to help him and they would just keep him comfortable. He is 86 years old and has had these problems for years. My problem, which was totally unexpected, was that I had to make the decision whether to resuscitate him or not. In spite of our AD's I found it impossible to say that we had decided against it. However, I was so very lucky because on Friday they said they would do an angiography. One artery was totally blocked but they managed

to get two stents in elsewhere. He had a quadruple by-pass 17 years ago, so he has been very lucky so far. I was sure I could cope when the time came but I found it far harder than expected to actually make the decision."

— Diane, USA

Do-Not-Resuscitate Orders

Many people are familiar with this expression, also known as DNR, DNAR (do not attempt resuscitation), or DNACPR (do not attempt cardiopulmonary resuscitation), but are not always aware of the effect of what having it, or not having it, means. This is a general introduction to the current state of these orders in England and Wales, Scotland and USA.

CPR (cardio pulmonary resuscitation) is an emergency procedure where one person presses up and down on the chest of the person who has suffered a heart attack, or cardiac arrest, and gives them a series of rescue breaths to help save their life. This person is often a medical professional. While CPR can be a life-saving measure, often when a person has an underlying condition, is already suffering a terminal illness, or is older, the odds of them leaving hospital alive are very small. For example, in the UK, for those with cancer that had spread to other parts of the body, the average percentage of those surviving CPR and then leaving hospital alive was just 1.9%. [14] In the USA every year, approximately 395,000 cases of cardiac arrest occur outside of a hospital setting, in which less than 6 percent survive. [15] More reasons to think about what you want towards the end of your life.

A valid DNR Order is a legal document which tells a medical team not to perform CPR on a patient. If the medical personnel know about this, then your heart will not be resuscitated if it has stopped. However, it is a big if, especially in an emergency situation, because medical personnel may not know about it. Hence it is up to you to ensure that you have communicated well to everyone concerned, and also have a way of identifying your wishes should you be involved in an emergency situation.

How to Tell People about My DNR

"I'm going to have a tattoo of DNR written on my chest," said my neighbour the other day. It's a common belief that this will mean you won't be resuscitated, but as a tattoo is not considered a legal document, this will not be enough. You need to have a DNR in place also, although a tattoo would perhaps mean in an emergency that at least the medic might ask to see the DNR. In the USA, when you are admitted to hospital as an outpatient, ER, or inpatient, you are asked when you register whether you have an AD and if you will provide a copy of it for your records. However, at home, you may wish to have your AD posted in a clear place for all to see (it might then even be a good talking point when you have a social gathering – nothing like creating opportunities to talk about this kind of thing!).

In various counties in England, an initiative has taken place (sometimes called the Green Cross Scheme, or Bottle In A Fridge) which involves keeping a plastic container (white with a green cross on it) inside your fridge door, containing a note to say you have an AD/AS/DNR and tells the medics where to find those documents. A white sticker with a green cross is then placed on the outside of your fridge door, and just inside the front door to your house to alert the medics that your instructions are there. Of course, this scheme entirely depends on the medics knowing to look out for that sticker; check if you have something similar in your state or county - or perhaps start one.

DNR's are usually provided in hospital by your doctor, when they need to know whether or not you wish your heart to be restarted if it stops. For example, when my husband was in hospital, and after he had been told there was nothing more they could do for him, he wanted to be transferred to a hospital nearer our home. Before this, a doctor asked if he would want his heart to be resuscitated if it should stop on the journey. He looked at me sadly and said no, which I believe was the right decision for him. In fact, I felt relieved. So the DNR order was signed (although it was never used as he ended up dying before he could be transferred). DNR's can also be provided by emergency medical providers or other health professionals, all who are legally obliged to respect your wishes as per the DNR Order.

In the USA, it is similar in that a DNR order is a legal order written in conjunction with a doctor that states that you do not want CPR, advanced cardiac life support or intubation if your heart or breathing should stop. However, your state will have different requirements in terms of signatures, witnessing etc., so you must check you are completing the correct document.

Essentially, without a DNR in place, medical professionals will attempt to restart your heart should it stop. If you do not want this, then you need to get your AD done, plus a DNR where appropriate.

CASE STORY: Polly

Polly, Celia Kitzinger's sister, was a keen gardener, an experienced sailor and on a weekend loved nothing more than pulling on her walking boots. However, in 2009 she was involved in a car crash, near to her home in Wales, and as a result suffered massive brain injuries. "We suspect she might well have died at the scene had an ambulance not been passing," says Celia. Polly received very quick treatment, but it was clear that her injuries were so severe there was not an awful lot which could be done. "We've always been the kind of family for whom subjects like death, politics and sex were discussed around the dinner table. We've always been very honest with each other and quite quickly we came to the realisation that whichever way you looked at it, the outcome for Polly was likely to be very grim."

They were also certain they knew what Polly's wishes would have been and in the early days and weeks after the crash they made various attempts to talk to doctors about the possible options. "Polly would not have wanted to live without quality of life, as she saw it. We all knew that. However, when we initially approached the medical team we were told it was too early to decide what to do. I'm still not sure what they meant."

Current guidelines state that following emergency treatment to stabilize a patient an assessment should be carried out to decide what, if any, future treatment is in their best interests. "We found it incredibly frustrating that we struggled to even find a doctor to talk to. Polly had worked in the mental health sector, she was passionate about standing up for people whose voices weren't being heard and whose rights were routinely overlooked. It was something of an irony that we found ourselves sat around her bedside looking at Polly who had been left in exactly that position."

Polly is now in a care home and will remain there to the end of her life. While she is conscious, she has multiple profound mental and physical disabilities and is unable to make any serious decisions about her own medical treatment.

"It's heart-breaking to see her like that when we know so absolutely that she wouldn't have wanted to live a life like that," says Celia. "Polly was always fiercely independent, but now she is wholly reliant on others. There is a tendency when people talk of someone in either a vegetative or semi-conscious state to picture someone in a Sleeping Beauty pose. That's just so far from the truth. Some moan, they thrash around, they gnash their teeth. Doctors will tell you that, if they are vegetative, they aren't suffering, but it doesn't look like that."

With Polly little more than a shell of the sister she had grown up with, Celia was prompted to write an Advance Decision. In the event of a worse case scenario, the document (which must include a sentence along the lines of 'I maintain these refusals even if my life is shortened as a result'; a signature; and be witnessed) is a legally binding refusal of treatment. If Polly had written one, the outcome for her could have been very different.[16]

Use of the AD

Your health and welfare power of attorney (in USA, sometimes called a healthcare proxy or health care agent) will use your AD to inform themselves about any decisions they may have to make on your behalf. So will your doctors. This means it will make it easier for them to make the right decision, and to feel good about doing so. The concern that they may not be doing the right thing is fully taken care of, so it works for everyone – you, your advocate, your family and friends, and your doctors.

It is not easy for medical professionals to have the responsibility for when someone should receive treatment or not. Every case is a person; everyone's situation is unique, and given similar circumstances, different decisions may be made for a variety of reasons. Thus an AD can be very useful to help the professionals, who will be able to discuss with you what treatment or non-treatment they recommend, why, and what are the outcomes of those. Sometimes, those in the medical profession are not always fully aware of what an AD is, and there have even been instances of confusing the DNR Order with the AD, and assuming that when someone has an AD that means they do not want to be resuscitated, should the occasion arise. Until such time as education on these matters has improved, it is up to you, in your personal situation, to inform those around you as best you can, including your doctors, carers, nurses, therapists, as well as family and friends.

"Some people think that the doctors know best, and that it's their decision, and that they will know what's best for you. Other people don't have that much respect for doctors, so I realize what goes in my AD is really down to me, and what I want; in discussion with others, of course."

— Sal, England

Preparing to Create an AD

There are various websites and organizations in most countries which will provide you with the necessary forms and advice to do this; please see the Resources section at the back for more information. However, there are certain things you can do first that will make the completion of these documents much easier.

Your Values

In order to be able to create an AD for yourself and feel good about it, it helps considerably if you are aware of what your values and beliefs about life and death are. Even if you feel sure about these, and even if you already have your AD, it is worth reading this section, because we change as we go through life, and what may have been important and relevant to you in your thirties or forties, may assume much less importance in your sixties, seventies or older. Being aware of your values is an ongoing process, and the decisions you make about your life and state of health at any time, including medical decisions, are based on the beliefs, preferences and values that matter most to you at that point.

Most important is to realize that your thoughts on this may change as a result of your circumstances. For instance, Stanley had written an AD, and then suffered a stroke at age 83. Doctors stated he would likely not live for more than a few days. His family prepared for him to die. As per the law in his country, he was however offered food and drink, which he started to take. This was seen as an indication that he wanted to live, and therefore by his actions he had over-ridden what he had said in his AD (which only comes into effect when someone is incapacitated, and unable to speak for themselves).

Knowing your values and beliefs can also provide important information for those who will have to make medical decisions for you if you are no longer able to do so This includes family, friends and physicians, as well as your welfare power of attorney. By talking about these issues ahead of time, and having your advance statement and end of life plan completed, family disagreements will be minimized, not to mention the reduction of possible arguments between families and doctors. Thus when such decisions do need to be made, the burden of responsibility may be lessened because others feel confident of your attitude towards treatment that prolongs life, and the reasons behind your written beliefs and decisions. Remember that it is easier to talk about these issues before a crisis occurs. Should it occur and you have communicated your wishes to another person, or have them written down and their location known, you'll be much more likely to be treated in a manner that is in line with what is important to you.

"My son, six years ago, had a terrible motorcycle accident. He was in ICU for forty-eight days. In that time, he had eight physical systems that were failing. The doctors said to me and his wife, 'Here's his Do-Not-Resuscitate document.' Because he had too many things wrong with him, the doctor said that the trend was downward. Finally, I said, 'The one system that is fine is the head. He has no neurological damage, he had his helmet on, so that is in good shape. So long as that's true, let's keep working to see if we can make some of these systems come back.'

Long story short, we did it, he came back, and he's fine now. When I talked to him about that decision, which I made for him, he is so grateful. It was based on, 'Is he still in there?' and 'Will he still be himself, regardless?' Because the doctors said things like 'Well, he'll be on dialysis for life,' and I said, 'So what, is he going to be in here? Is he going to be himself? Is he going to be able to function in the world?'

As it turns out, of course, they were all wrong. He still has trouble with some things, but he's a person still, and he loves life, and there's no reason why he shouldn't live a long time. So when you look at questions such as, 'Should they feed me? Should they not feed me?', I would say that as long as my personhood is still in there, whatever else is going on outside me, I can probably have a good quality of life. So I leave it to my heirs to think about that, and to ask it ahead of time, should I ever be in that kind of situation. It was so amazing to have this experience with my son. Now he knows what to ask in relation to me."

— Diane, Canada

To help you in discovering your own values and beliefs about treatment at the end of life, look at the statements below and see which ones you can easily answer. Use them as a basis on which to have a conversation with a relevant person; write your answers down for yourself (and perhaps others) to see clearly; or simply to make sure your power of attorney, next of kin, and spouse/partner or other person are aware of how you feel.

Life in General

- Do you have any goals for the future? If so, what are they?
- How satisfied are you with what you have achieved in your life, on a scale of 1–10, where 10 is completely satisfied?
- What, for you, makes life worth living? Name the top three things.
- What are you most afraid of?
- Do you have particular activities you enjoy (e.g., hobbies, watching TV, reading, listening to music, painting, crafting etc.)?

Health

- How would you describe your current state of health?
- How do any health problems or disabilities affect you, your work and your ability to function on a day to day basis? Do they affect your family and if so, how?
- How do you feel about these problems or disabilities? What would you like others to know about this?
- Do you have difficulties with basic life activities such as eating, preparing food, sleeping, dressing, bathing, etc.?

Being a Burden: Self-sufficiency and Independence

- How do you feel about being dependent on someone else for your care needs?
- Does independence or dependence already affect your life, and if so, how?
- If your current physical or mental health gets worse, how would you feel about your independence and ability to be self-sufficient?
- Does the thought of being a burden to your family trouble you and if so, what would you like to have happen to lessen that?

Personal Relationships

- What role do family and friends play in your life, and how important are they to you?
- How do you expect friends, family and others to support your decisions regarding any medical treatment you may need now or in the future?

Religious and/or Spiritual Beliefs

- Do you have a spiritual/religious background or beliefs that are important to you?
- How do your beliefs affect your feelings toward serious, chronic or terminal illness?
- Is there a community of some kind that supports you in your beliefs? How would they do that?
- Given your beliefs, what is important to you about your end of life care?

How You Live

- Have you lived alone or with others over the last 10 years?
- Is living alone important to you, or do you prefer company?
- How might illness, disability or age affect where you currently live?
- Would a nursing home or other residential facility be acceptable to you, or not?
- Are there any other general comments you'd like to make about what's important about where you live?

Relationships with Doctors, Nurses and Other Health Professionals

- How do you relate to your doctors? Do you trust them, respect their decisions, feel like they give you enough time?
- Do you want their decisions to be respected over and above how your family feel?
- How do you feel about other caregivers, including doctors, nurses, therapists, chaplains, social workers, etc.?

It's Impossible to Decide!

"I'm finding all these decisions very difficult because I have no idea exactly how I'd like my end of life to go because I don't know how it's going to happen. I've only got very general things when I think about it and even those, I might want to change at the actual time. It's quite a difficult one to confront."

— Richard, England

It may feel just impossible to make these decisions. However, if you don't make a decision to complete your AD, then by default you are making a decision to accept whatever happens, no matter what. That includes doctors making a decision for you, which may not be in agreement with what your family want for you, or what you would have wanted. This may be okay with you, there is no right or wrong here. However, at the very least you will be making that decision consciously. If you decide not to make an AD, then you can record that information. Should the relevant people need to know about this, understanding that you considered it and made a decision not to have one will be very helpful for them, whether or not they agree with it.

One of the reasons it is impossible is because we have to put ourselves into a situation where we don't really know how we're going to want to be, or how we might respond, until it actually happens. With this kind of thing, of course, we hope that it doesn't happen. The best that you can do is consider these things beforehand, and get as clear as you can. Given that it could happen any moment, this really is a time to consider this statement:

- If I was in this situation yesterday (incapacitated and unable to make health decisions for myself), what would I be wanting to happen today?

If nothing else, this question focuses the mind on what you want to do in your life before you may not be able to do it anymore! That then highlights the need to keep your AD updated, because as you get older, your values change.

Remember, this document is like an insurance policy. You (of course) hope that it will never be needed, but just in case, you have the information available. You wouldn't consider not having car or house insurance, so why not this, which is arguably even more important, and certainly cheaper? So consider these questions for your AD and Advance Statement from wherever you are now in your life (because you never know what might happen), and also note that you need to review both documents, and update them, regularly, along with any other end of life documents you need to review, like your will.

If it is taking you time to come to terms with creating your AD, acknowledge it, accept that is happening, and have that be okay. Remember there is no point in adding another layer by feeling guilty because you 'should' be doing it. That will just make it even more likely that you won't get to it! Step by step, even just answering one of the questions to do with your AD each day, or each week, is a lot better than nothing, and if you need help you can reach out to a local organization, or of course to **www.beforeigosolutions.com**

> "My husband and I have a joint will, but when it comes to our advance directives, we feel differently, and so I'm going to fill out an advance directive form and make him fill out one too. It's because he has a more pessimistic view of life, and he isn't going to want more support, like I would."
>
> — Diane, USA

Anticipatory Care Plans (UK only)

This document states in detail what kind of healthcare you would like to receive towards the end of your life. Depending on your medical condition this could be a matter of years, months or weeks. It is similar in some ways to the *Before I Go Workbook*, but goes into much more depth for those with current medical conditions (e.g., what kind of medication you are on). It is an excellent document to be part of your overall end of life plan, if something of this nature is available in your country. Ask your local GP for information.

POLST (Provider Orders for Life-Sustaining Treatment) (USA only)

This is similar to an ACP in that it is a document that allows a conversation between a provider and a patient with a serious illness towards the end of life to create specific medical orders. These would be honoured by health care workers during any kind of medical crisis. A POLST form allows emergency medical services to provide treatment that is wanted before possibly transporting a patient to an emergency facility. It exists in some states only, so check out the situation in your state.

Video Advance Directives

There is a movement in the USA that states that the use of a video testimonial to an AD or a POLST form can help prevent mistakes in interpretation regarding the choice of life-sustaining treatments, or allowing the natural process of death to happen. Studies have shown that the kind of mistakes that can occur result in preventing the natural dying process, or leading to overuse of costly medical resources. However, the results also showed that when video testimonials attached to the AD or POLST were viewed, there was a higher level of agreement (95%) between doctors as to what the patient's wishes were. To learn more about making a video testimonial of this nature, see Resources Section.

The basic message of this chapter is: start the process of getting your AD and advance statement completed, and keep going until it is done, signed and witnessed. Include your photo, and perhaps consider a video testimonial of yourself stating your wishes.

• • •

Now it's time for another pause – if you have actually completed your AD, you can give yourself a big pat on the back! And maybe make it a cause for a proper celebration. It is a huge thing when you get this kind of documentation finally organized, so it deserves acknowledgement. Even if you have only completed some of the steps, they also require acknowledgment – just make sure you keep on going until you complete everything that is required. And then take the opportunity to attune once more before you continue reading.

Financial Affairs

This is one subject that often has people turning away, with heart sinking and a promise to themselves that they will get round to doing something about it; and then it never happens.

Here's why it is so important to make sure your financial affairs are not only in good order, but that you have detailed what you want to happen with your finances after your death.

1. It makes it much easier for your executor if they know where you keep all your financial information.

2. Itemising all your accounts/insurances/benefits/pensions means it is easy for them to access, and your executor won't be left wondering if there is anything that hasn't been discovered.

3. It increases the likelihood that your financial wishes will be taken care of in the way you detailed.

4. It minimizes family arguments.

5. It saves time and money for your family that would otherwise be spent on trying to sort out muddles.

The most important thing you can do regarding your financial affairs is to include your wishes in an up-to-date will. If you want to ensure your money and anything else of import goes to the person, people, charity or cause that you want, then you need to write a will detailing this. Otherwise, the law in your country or state will determine to whom your assets will go, and this may not be whom you want it to be. Even if, for whatever reason, you decide not to have a will, it is better to write down your wishes, because there is still more chance of them then being carried out than if you hadn't written anything down at all.

Regarding the financial implications of a will, it is not unusual for families who normally get on well to find their emotions running high if they perceive their siblings have been treated differently, or to be left with feelings of bitterness and/or resentment after a loved family member has died, particularly parents. They may even dispute a will. It is as if without the parents steering the helm of the family ship, the crew, in their grief, discover long-held family patterns from childhood that come to the surface to get re-enacted.

Even if you can't imagine that this would ever happen, it can, and it does. The best way you can minimize this kind of thing happening is to detail your wishes in a will, and stick to them. Even then, wills can get contested but it is still much better to have one than not.

"After one of my best friends died suddenly, aged only 51, her mother had a nightmare. Her daughter's phone and computer were password protected and they had to deal with the mess of her affairs. They didn't even know if she had a will. It's made a terrible time even more stressful. I heard later that the situation became much worse and ended very badly. The only signed will they eventually could find was one from when my friend was still in a toxic marriage, which ended a decade before she died. Half of her estate was left to her husband.

Legally he couldn't inherit as the law treats an ex-spouse as deceased but his heirs were entitled to his share. His two sisters, who were vile to her for many years, and whom she couldn't stand, inherited several hundred thousand pounds. Her own brother got nothing. Her mother was enraged and distressed but didn't want the estate to disappear in legal fees, plus she wasn't in any state to go to court and contest it. It was horrible.

At no point did the two sisters get in touch, send condolences, say thank you, offer to take a lesser sum or offer to donate some to charity. They just took the money. Hard as I try not to be judgemental, I can't quite manage it. Her not having a will and clear financial affairs made a shocking death so much worse for the family."

— Caroline, England

Who Currently Handles Your Money?

If you use an accountant, financial adviser, insurance planner or adviser, and any investment fund managers or tax specialists, these people (or firms) should be named in your plan, with contact details. If you have no-one, perhaps because you have little money or assets to leave, then make sure you state that. Some people prefer to detail everything on an Excel spreadsheet, others to simply list accounts on a piece of paper. Still others prefer to use an online platform. Whatever you decide to do, keep it simple, clear and concise.

> "My parents are pretty well organized when it comes to their finances, and they have stated very simply in writing that each account or monetary arrangement of any kind has a file in the top drawer of the filing cabinet. I've seen them, and though it might be helpful if all these were listed on one piece of paper, it will not be onerous for me to go through the top drawer when the time comes."
>
> — Sandy, Scotland

Think about the kind of person you are, and what filing arrangement suits you best (whether online or offline). So long as your executor knows where to find this information, and how to access it if it is online, then you are doing fine. Make sure you document the location of everything, as a minimum. If you don't have any of the stated documentation (because it is irrelevant), make sure you state that too.

Debts

You may want to ensure that all unsecured debts, i.e., credit cards or personal loans, are paid off, if this is affordable and practical. It simplifies things for your executor if this is the case, and that of course means that any money or belongings that you have gifted in your will won't take so long to get to where you have chosen them to go. If debts still exist after you die, in the UK and USA, these may be paid out of your estate. Unless you had a joint loan or agreement, or provided a loan guarantee, you are not responsible for a husband, wife's or civil partner's debts, but that does not mean that a credit card company, for instance, would not come after you for what they are owed.

Generally, if there are debts, assets will be sold to pay these off and this could limit the amounts of money or assets going to where you had directed you wanted them to go. A Scottish lawyer told me that she had a situation where the husband had been expected to die and therefore had time to do some planning. Unfortunately, a financial adviser had told him that his debts would die with him. He ran up huge credit card bills in his last few months, and his wife is now in the position where she will either have to do an equity release from their house (a very expensive way of paying off debts) or sell the family home. So it is much better if you can tidy this up before you die, and not leave any debt; but also check the situation with your own lawyer and financial adviser in your country or state.

Life insurance is one manageable way in which you may be able to provide for any debts after you die, and about which you can do something now, if you don't already have it. Alternatively, you can set aside an account into which you pay regularly, and stipulate this is to be used to clear any debts, pay for your funeral, or any other costs that are relevant, or that might arise. If you have an executor, they will be legally bound to carry out your wishes. If you don't, but still state your wishes as to this in writing, then it may or may not happen.

Your Financial Power of Attorney

You may choose the same person or people for this as for your health and welfare POA, or a different person or people. All the information relating to POA in that section applies here. However, it makes sense to choose someone for this role who has a head for figures, and whom you trust to make good financial decisions on your behalf, and whom you respect.

Trusts for Financial Matters

These are different in different countries and states, so if you want to find out the best options for your particular situation, then you must take professional advice. You can get this initially through an accountant or lawyer; and you may be able to do this for free, depending on what free legal advice offers you have associated with whatever societies, charities or membership sites to which you belong. Do some basic homework first, before you make an expensive appointment with a professional.

There are many areas to be covered under the topic of finances. Here are some of the most important ones:

- Pensions and Annuity Documentation
- Insurances of all kinds
- Life Policies
- Mobile Phone Companies
- Energy Utility Companies
- Accounts and deeds of all properties, including home, rental and holiday properties
- Stock and Share certificates

Please don't let your financial affairs documentation overwhelm you! If even the thought of your finances makes you yawn, or feels daunting in any way, read the Chapter on Obstacles to Taking Action, and implement some of the tactics there. Remember to take it step by little step. That is how you get to the top of a mountain – and that is also how you come to the end of any project or task.

10

Practical Household Matters

●●●●●●

"To the well-organized mind, death is but the next great adventure."

— JK ROWLING, British novelist/screenwriter, b. 1965

ATTUNEMENT: Take a pause. After reading this paragraph, just close your eyes and notice your breathing, and how your body feels. Reflect on your thoughts about household matters.

Your House or Home

It is very easy to underestimate how important this section is. In the face of everything else, does it really matter whether those left behind know how your household runs? Well, as it turns out, it does. Why? Because of what I mentioned earlier about the effects of grief. My husband and I had covered many questions, but not all. Here's one way I found out about household practicalities.

Philip died on 1st December 2011, and I had a friend come to stay with me over Christmas and New Year. She and I made the best of the holiday season and she had returned that afternoon on the flight to England. I drove slowly home, only too aware that now, after the distractions of the funeral, Christmas and New Year, there really was a new beginning for me, no matter how much I didn't want it. I entered through the front door, heavily aware that silence greeted me. I had planned to do some work, which I did and later on, I sat down and flicked on the television. The familiar screen I expected was not there. In its place were instructions that I didn't understand. I exasperatedly pressed a few buttons, hesitating in case I wouldn't be able to find my way back even to this screen. No luck. I found the instruction booklet in the drawer beneath the telly, but it was worse; full of endless pages telling me all sorts of things I didn't need to know. I burst into tears. I just needed Philip; he would have known what to do.

I know this sounds not very feminist and independent; I know it sounds even a bit pathetic, but the thing is, especially if you are part of a couple, you tend to have roles. Think about it, not each of you knows everything about how the household works. It doesn't make sense to do that when there are always so many things to be engaged with in family life. One of you is likely to know more about the garden than the other; or know more about the workings of the kitchen than the other. It used to be common that men held the purse strings and women didn't know how to write a cheque, and so really were at sea if their husband died first.

Nowadays, that doesn't happen so much, but even in a straw poll research I did amongst my friends, I was amazed to discover how many individuals in a couple did not know things like insurance renewal dates, or even where to find the insurance documents; didn't know how the washing machine worked or didn't understand the burglar alarm system. So it was with me and the TV – if only we had taken the time for him to write down some simple instructions for me regarding the TV operation. Instruction manuals today are so complex, and often online – all I needed was a simple flow chart to find the channels I most wanted. However, 'if only's' really don't work. They serve instead to prolong the feelings, to emphasize the pain, to cause a plague of questions. None of this helped though, in the moment. Rather, I just bawled my eyes out, wailing loudly to the empty house, and feeling foolish on top, because of the silliness of the situation. Eventually, the tears stopped, and I rang a neighbour to come and help me with the telly.

All this kind of thing can be avoided if you are willing, right now, to answer questions to do with the running of your household. Here are just a few of them:

- Where are the washing machine/other appliance instructions?
- Do you know how to operate the heating system controls?
- Can you operate the oven/lawnmower/other appliance?
- Do you know the combinations to any briefcases?
- Do you know where the mains water tap is?

Remember to bear in mind the thought, 'If I had died yesterday, what would I have wanted to be in place?'

To help you with this, take a walk around your house. (All houses, if you have more than one property.) Go into every room, look at it with eyes of a newcomer seeing it for the first time, and ask yourself:

'What happens in this room that I know about that no-one else does?'

CASE STORY: Hugh and Janet

We had been saying for ages this would be a good idea. Looking into the myriad different aspects on everything that deserves consideration seemed daunting at first. But going through the *Before I Go Workbook* alongside others helped us to reflect on what is most important for us, and then to make a start. It was revealing to see how different the requirements of each workshop participant were. Yet listening to their concerns and comments really helped us clarify our own needs.

We discovered how important it was to explore what each of us needed to know about continuing life without our partner. It is so easy to remain ignorant of key information our partner holds for us – where the fuse boxes or stop-cocks are; what important documents we have, and where to find them; and so on.

Discussing everything from how to operate the central heating system, to what preferences, if any, we had on how our burial/ final celebration might look has brought on a depth of intimacy between us, that on its own is worthwhile experiencing. Looking at the possibility of incapacity, and death for either one of us has not been the dreadful subject one could imagine. Now the ball is rolling it feels good and positive.

— Hugh and Janet, Scotland

If you live alone, still do the same process. Someone will come to your house after you have died, and will need to know information about how it works. Even small things like what days the rubbish is collected is useful. It's not absolutely necessary, as often neighbours can fill in details like this, but it is very helpful. Simply identify the systems, structures or belongings that you have taken for granted because they've been there so long you don't notice them anymore, or because someone else deals with them instead of you. You could invite a single friend to do this with you, and then return the favour to them.

Vehicles

It may be you consider that providing detailed information about your vehicles is not necessary. For instance, is it really essential to know the tyre pressures of the family car? Of course not! You can easily find that out by going online, asking your local mechanic, looking in the car handbook.

However, remember that when people are grieving they are often not thinking straight, and those left behind may well be in this state of mind. It may not occur to them to ask anyone, or research information. The last thing they may want to do is approach a neighbour or even a friend. That's what happened to me – it took me ages before it dawned that I could look in the car handbook to discover what the tyre pressures were. It never occurred to me to ask the mechanic in the garage. I was stuck in a place of feeling sorry for myself around the car because now I had to look after it all myself, when it had been Philip's role previously.

So remember, these questions are all about you making life as easy for your loved ones as possible, in a time of high emotion and turmoil as routines, rhythm and right-thinking all get turned upside down.

Decluttering Your Home

One of the things that has raised its head in the *Before I Go* groups is the need for decluttering, in this context sometimes known as 'death cleaning'. This can be anything from keeping things tidy, to a full-blown admittance that you are a hoarder, and then every level in-between. If you recognize you are out of control with this, then it is time to get some help. One person told me she moved house in an attempt to deal with the amount of stuff she had, only to move all the stuff with her.

If you recognize yourself in this scenario, then it will benefit you enormously to get help. This simply could be a regular arrangement with a friend, but if you are emotionally unable to give away stacks of papers from 30 years ago, then something else is at play here, and you need professional help. Contact a local counsellor, or a clutter clearance expert with experience of this kind of thing.

If on the other hand, you simply see that you have just too much stuff and you *can* get rid of it, but haven't done so, then it is time to take some steps to have this happen. Here's a few tips on this, from someone who has moved 26 times in her life and has been forced to let go of 'stuff' each time; and who keeps topped up with regular purging of her stuff!

- Choose a small area of your house or a specific task to focus on: e.g., a drawer to clear out, a folder to sort out, a shelf, or a corner of a room.
- Make a decision to get that done by a deadline that you set yourself. Commit to doing it.

- Start doing it by sorting things into one of these categories:
  - *Useful? Put it into a space designated for that thing, or create a space for it and put it there.*
  - *Beautiful or brings you joy? Love the fact that you are keeping it and create a space for it.*
  - *Love it for another reason? Know why that is, feel good about it, and choose to display it or store it, and then create the space for it.*
  - *Celebrate that you have taken action.*

Refer to Obstacle No. 6 in the Obstacles Chapter for more information on decluttering.

11

Family, Friends, and Personal Information

• • • • • •

"It is good to have a reminder of death before us, for it helps us to understand the impermanence of life on this Earth, and this understanding may aid us in preparing for our own death. He who is well prepared is he who knows that he is nothing compared with Wakan-Tanka, who is everything; then he knows that world which is real."

— **BLACK ELK**, Native American Indian, 1863-1950

ATTUNEMENT: Take a pause. After reading this paragraph, just close your eyes and notice your breathing, and how your body feels. Give yourself a moment or two, then reflect on your thoughts about your family and friends in relation to your death.

The people to list here in your end of life plan are those who are the most important to you. This will include your executor, those who are to receive a copy of your plan, and any others whom you consider need to be told immediately what is going on. This may or may not include your blood family – not everyone feels as close to blood relatives as they do to dear friends. Your children or partner may not know who your close friends were, so thinking about who is in *your* life is vital, as is naming them and including their contact details.

In these days of different ways to contact people, and where people keep their contacts lists, you may find there are several different places to be identified as to how these people may be notified. If you have all your contacts in a phone, write that down (and make sure that in your list of passwords, you have stated your phone password). If you have a physical address book, state where it is.

"I've been spending time this evening making a contact list of all the folks whom I would want to receive a phone call when I die. It is such a fascinating activity! It's really clear that some folks – closest friends and family – would receive a call. But then there are dozens of people who fall into a category I call 'strangers-between-the-cracks'. I would hate for them to find out on FB ... and yet we also aren't *best* friends. So one thing I started doing is categorizing people into a phone tree and trying to choose one person from each 'tribe' who might then connect with some others who are all in the same group – like college friends, for instance. Just doing this one thing is such a relief!! I've meant to do this for years. I can see how easy this will make it having all this in one place!"

– Sherry, USA

Personal Information

Make sure this section covers all the information that is personal to you. For instance, include your NHS or social security numbers, your passport number, your driving licence number as just some of those administrative details that make life easier when they are all in one place. You would put here important dates too (family members birthdates, for example) and those that have been special to you, like when you received a particular award or had an unusual travel trip or sabbatical.

Leave a Living Legacy

A living legacy is a phrase that covers quite a few things. Often we associate the word 'legacy' with a monetary gift to a charity or other cause, paid out after we die. Indeed, the Oxford English dictionary describes it as: 'An amount of money or property left to someone in a will'. Many people leave a legacy in this way, providing for a grandchild's education, donating to a cause they were passionate about during their lives, or gifting a property or other asset to a foundation. However, the dictionary also states 'something left or handed down by a predecessor', and although this is more commonly thought of as (in their example) 'the legacy of centuries of neglect', a Living Legacy is something quite different.

A Living Legacy is a gift that you create while you are alive and becomes fully appreciated after you have died. It is about the essence of who you are, and continues long after you have died, and in any kind of form you like. It is something that demonstrates your values, beliefs, attitudes, wishes, memories, desires, hopes, love, advice and blessings. It could be that you choose to be remembered in it for your acts of charity, for being a good listener, or being inspirational in the way you dealt with adversity. It's about whom you have influenced, and who's influenced you, and whose lives you have touched and how. It is something that can be picked up and from which others can get a sense of you – words they can read, a video to watch, or the sound of your voice; the opportunity to touch items that have been important to you, and to know the reason why. The smell of an item that you often wore close to your heart. A living legacy can also be a combination of lessons you have learned during your life, important events that helped to shape you; memories, traditions and sentiments and why they were important, and of course, all bound up in stories.

It's only too often after our parents, or someone in the older generation of the family dies, that we realize too late all those questions to which only they would know the answer. How many have said, 'I wish X was still here, they would be able to explain that' or, 'If only Y were still alive, then I could ask them.' However, we don't take care of this, either in asking the questions of the older members of our family, or encouraging them to record their lives in any way. Thus we end up with detailed family trees but not very many of the stories of someone's life. Or plenty of old black and white photos, but no names or dates on them. These then get chucked out, because it's not the facts that are so important as the stories and the legends they create, and the impact they have on other family members and friends.

A living legacy therefore enables you to create the story of your life as you are living it. It lets you highlight the points in your life, where, if you had made another decision, your life would have turned out quite differently. It means you can pass on words of wisdom and advice to the younger generation, your grandchildren and great-grandchildren; or to younger members of your community, and to share your sense of humour, hopes and wishes, and ensures that a part of you lives on well beyond your physical lifetime.

"I was fortunate enough to type up my mother's memoirs, earlier this year. She had gone to a University of Third Age creative group for writing your life story. There was a huge pad of papers, and she says, 'you'll type it up, won't you?' and I said, 'yes, yes, of course I will'... and didn't. She's 94 now, and getting frail. I really needed to do this. I typed it up – all fifty-thousand words of it. And I was able to print it out, and give it to her, while she was still able to read it and enjoy revisiting the memories she had begun to forget. Now I don't have that guilt of not having done it."

— Christina, England

The desire to leave a legacy is common. Many people see the effect of their own lives living on through their children, and of course that is one wonderful way to leave your mark on the world, but there are others too. I remember when I realized I was not going to be able to have children, it became very important to me that my life made an impact in some other way than through a child. About a year after this realization, I published my first book, *Choose Your Thoughts, Change Your Life* (now out of print). I referred to it at the time as 'my child'. I even used the words, 'I want to leave a legacy of something good to show that I existed.'

So it is a timeless and common desire to leave a legacy of meaning and purpose, in whatever shape and form. It taps into our beliefs that we are part of something bigger, and our need to live a life of purpose.

"I realized I have a collection of my writings. I have a whole load of genealogy stuff I want somebody to be executor of. I'll have to ask through the family to see who wants to be the caretaker of it all – which of the grandkids, or the great grandkids for that matter, will care for and expand the genealogy research and the associated stories, and keep it available for more generations to come."

— Diane, Canada

Creating your Living Legacy can feel like a rather overwhelming project to undertake so here's a few questions to answer to get you going:

- What are your favourite books, jokes, poems, pieces of music, recipes?
- What are you most proud of in your life so far?
- What was the greatest challenge in your life so far?
- How would you sum up your life?
- How would you describe love?

Decide if you want to write your legacy, use video or recordings, make a physical creation, be interviewed, use keep-sake photos, make a DVD; or let your imagination run wild and come up with something unique to you, created using all or some of these methods, or other things that come to mind. And remember to enjoy yourself while you are doing it! Your Living Legacy can be as small or as big as you like. It can also include writing birthday cards or for other occasions in advance, to be opened on that day. This is especially good for children, but it works for any age. A Living Legacy can be a lovely gift to those left behind, but if you want to do it, it requires thinking about now. There's no right or wrong about this; there's no good or bad, or judgment about it at all. Never underestimate the comforting power of leaving behind a Living Legacy – if you're interested in starting this, or continuing where you left off, then check out what is going on around Living Legacies, at **www.beforeigosolutions.com**

Secrets

If you know somebody is likely to find out something about you, or your family, by going through your stuff after you die, and it may be harmful in some way, then you need to take care of this in plenty of time. A friend of mine with a terminal illness decided she was going to burn all her journals. That was a lot of journals over a 50-year period; she had kept them all. She decided she didn't want her children, or her grandchildren to know about all these writings. So she had a big bonfire of her journals, and felt amazing doing it. She hadn't expected to feel so 'released' by this action. If you have this kind of information, whether in actual journals or on your computer, consider whether what is in them really needs to be read by anyone after you have gone. If you want it read, why not when you are alive? Make a conscious decision about this.

If you are the holder of an actual secret in your family or amongst your friends, it's important to realize that if you die without this being told to anyone else, then that secret will die with you. That is not necessarily a problem, however; from my therapeutic background, I have seen how a secret can filter down through generation to generation, with nobody really understanding why the family dynamics are the way they are. It can often feel like there is a missing piece of the puzzle, which when it is found explains a lot of family patterns and behaviour. So it is important you make a conscious decision about this. To help you do this, ask yourself questions such as:

- If this secret dies with me, what effect might that have, if any?
- Is there anyone I need to speak to about anything?
- Is there something that only I know (even if I don't think of it as a secret) that needs to be told to someone else?

- Who would benefit from being told this?
- Who would it harm?

If you choose to communicate about a secret, then you don't have to say it before you die. You could write it down, only to be opened after your death, and by a particular person. You could tell someone else whom you trust not to say anything until you authorize it, or until after a particular person has died. It really doesn't matter how you take action around this, so long as you make a conscious decision.

CASE STORY: Amanda

Sally and Robert had two boys, Simon and Hugh. Simon was married to his second wife, Lucy, and together they had a child, Natasha, Sally's grand-daughter. Sally and Lucy had quite a typical daughter-in-law/mother-in-law relationship, and didn't quite see eye to eye, and although Sally tried to keep an open house for the family, popping in and out of each other's houses with ease never really happened.

Christmas is often a challenging time for families, and Sally was the kind of woman who gave a lot of thought to all family members. One Christmas she bought her daughter-in-law a thoughtful and quite expensive gift. In return, she received from Lucy a small, inexpensive trinket. Sally told her favourite niece, Amanda, about this incident, and also then her son Simon, saying she felt disappointed, hurt and slighted. Simon then told his wife. The result of this was a series of emails backwards and forwards between the two women, ending in an email from Lucy to her mother-in-law, stating that she had no right to be alive, and she wished it was Sally who had died, and not her own mother the previous year.

Sadly Sally did die, the following year, but not before she had made her husband and second son Hugh promise not to tell anyone about the interchange of emails. Lucy had not told her husband Simon either.

A couple of years later, Amanda was at a family gathering and met her cousin Simon. He brought up the subject of his Dad Robert, feeling perplexed and cross that his father didn't have much of a relationship with his grand-daughter, nor him and his wife.

Amanda had to make a decision about whether or not to tell the secret that she knew. Sally's husband and second son had been sworn to secrecy, but she had not. She decided to tell Simon what had happened between his mother and his wife, saying that she couldn't let Simon continue to think that his Dad was an awful grandparent.

Simon was stunned. Everything fell into place and he finally was able to understand why his family were all keeping their distance from him, his wife and daughter. But the shock of discovering his wife had not told him, and that she had behaved in such a manner, made him consider leaving his marriage.

In the end, he did not leave Lucy, and it all came out into the open after Simon spoke with her about this. The family are still together, and Simon and his father are much closer. But the family suffered damage – the situation has not been forgotten even though the marriage is still intact. They rarely are part of wider family occasions now, which means that their daughter Natasha also is suffering the effects of her mother's behaviour and her grandmother's desire to keep it all secret.

— Amanda, England

This story illustrates how very difficult the keeping or not keeping of secrets is. On balance I would say it is always better to have them out in the open – but it depends on the circumstances, who is going to be hurt, and whether or not it is important enough to hurt those who are living. Clearly in this situation the effect of the email exchange, Sally's demand that it all be kept a secret, and her husband and son's keeping of it, was damaging the continuing family relationships.

Secrets manifest themselves in all sorts of other ways, too. Families are not perfect, people do make mistakes, forgiveness is part of being alive. There are several things to think about if you are the one who knows a secret, or indeed if you are someone who wishes others to keep a secret.

Five Lessons about Secrets

1. **Never use Social Media**, texts, emails or anything else to write any emotion-based messages. You cannot determine how the other person will read them. If it is not something you can say to them in person, then don't say it at all.

2. **Be wary of asking others to keep a secret.** To honour you they may do it, but you put a huge onus on them by requesting this. The effect of asking someone to keep a secret can last for generations and generations.

3. **Be wary of keeping something secret yourself.** A true secret will be known by you and not by anyone else, certainly not anyone who might be near to those concerned. When Sally told her husband and one son about the email messages, she was setting up the situation that eventually happened. In a situation like this one in the case study, the hurt was so great that Sally just had to tell someone, and not surprisingly it was her husband. What might have been better was to find a way to address the mother-in-law/daughter-in-law relationship directly, and then the inadvertent collusion by husband and younger son would have been foiled.

4. **Never underestimate family relationships.** They are complex, interwoven and full of feelings, often. Even if you think they are not. Ignore this at your peril!

5. **Keep your relationships up to date** – by that I mean be brave and speak of small things that make you feel uncomfortable, so they don't have the chance to grow further. Nip them in the bud, and you will likely increase your chances of a good relationship with that person. Alternatively, let it roll off your back. Not easy, but not impossible either.

In the case story, Amanda made a courageous decision in deciding to tell the secret, but you can see why there's not a right or wrong answer. That's why it's such a personal thing, but it really warrants talking and thinking about it, and I would highly recommend that. Get professional help if you need to talk it through with someone. If you have no secrets, nothing that might jump out of the closet after your death, you might even state that, as in 'I haven't got any secrets'. You don't want anyone left wondering, and worrying about what they might find.

12

Last Days' Wishes

······

"Life is pleasant. Death is peaceful.
It's the transition that's troublesome."

— ISAAC ASIMOV, American sci-fi writer, 1920-1992

ATTUNEMENT: Take a pause. After reading this paragraph, just close your eyes and notice your breathing, and how your body feels. Reflect on your immediate thoughts about what you might want during your last days. Notice you may get caught up in thoughts such as 'But how will I know? I don't even know where I will be' and so on. No need to engage with these thoughts, simply notice them and come back to imagining what your ideal situation may be, given where you are now in your life.

This section refers to the weeks up to the point of death. The term 'palliative care' is often used at this point, i.e., when the medics have realized there is nothing more they can do, and you just are to be kept comfortable until the end. But how does anyone know when that is? It is really hard to say, although professionals or those who have been around many dying people will often see signs such as skin becoming mottled, or breathing changes. What is really important here are the other people you would like to have around at this point, the people you don't want to be around, and your willingness to write this down so people know in advance.

People You Want around You

When I asked my husband the question 'Who would you like around you in your last days?', he reeled off quite a lot of names of people he wanted by his bed, and then we laughed as we realized they probably wouldn't all fit in the room. At that stage we didn't know where he would be, but his preference was to die at home, so our bedroom was where we imagined these people, and it wasn't that big. We made a list of ideal people, and then the essential ones, who were me, and his oldest friend from Los Angeles.

"I had a very sociable dear friend who, before she died aged 30, had a conversation with her parents about who she wanted around her. She listed probably 10 or 20 people. Her parents were very private, but when they understood why it was important for Dominique to have all those people there, they found it challenging as they had hoped it would be more private. But knowing that it was important for Dominique at the end of her life to have all these people, they found they could facilitate this. Once she passed away her parents spent time with their daughter alone, but again it was the conversation beforehand that made all the difference."

— Lyall, France

People You Don't Want around You

As well as having who you want around you in the last days, it's equally important to be conscious of who you might not want to have there. If someone comes to mind when you read this sentence, notice how you feel about writing that name down. When I was talking with a private client about this he was concerned his sister-in-law would be there, and he really didn't want her to be. That decision hasn't yet been written down, but it's been raised and is now in his consciousness, which is important because in time it has much more chance of being addressed.

It takes courage to write names down, or even just to tell someone, but this is your last days we are talking about. While writing down what you want will also serve your nearest and dearest, ultimately it's a time to put yourself first, not be too worried about upsetting others, and do the very best you can to live this last period in as self-loving a manner as possible.

"Clergy of any kind are a big turnoff for me, so I added that in my workbook. People who know me understand my spirit and my connection to nature so under my list of 'atmosphere' I'm putting some connection to nature. If I can't have a tree in my room, take me out under the trees if possible."

— Diane, USA

Location

Did you know that most people say they want to die at home, but that most die in hospital? According to research from the Sue Ryder organization in the UK, 63% say they want to die at home, but only 20.8% do actually die there. [17] In fact, most people (54.8%) die in hospital. In the USA, a Stanford School of Medicine report states that approximately 80% of Americans would prefer to die at home, but only 20% actually do so, with 60% dying in acute care hospitals, and 20% in nursing homes. [18]

At the very least, if you know where you would want to die (given the choice), you need to tell someone. Even one person is better than no-one. Ideally, you would complete your plan, have an advance directive (see Chapter 9), and have all members of your family know what you want. This is crucial, because the doctors also need to know and if you haven't told them, it is much less likely to happen. This also ties in with your welfare power of attorney (see Chapter 9), so make sure you have that set up too.

What is important for those you leave behind is that they know what you wanted, just like in any other area of your end of life care. In some countries, you have to apply for hospice care. In others, you enter into a building called a hospice, whilst others have hospice care at home, or a mixture of all these. In other words you need to think about it beforehand, do some research, make a decision and write it down.

> "I wonder how easy it would be for people to support me in my own home, because the place you think is very comfortable and supportive for you right now might turn out to be totally the opposite if it's not possible to easily manage your situation. Then the whole point of being at home would be totally undermined."
> — Richard, England

If you know you want to die at home, it is worthwhile writing the address down too, just in case you end up in a situation where no-one knows what you meant by home. (This also highlights the fact that your plan is a 'living and breathing document' and needs to be regularly updated, unless you don't mind that what you wanted to have happen years ago still happens today.)

Other Things to Consider in Your Last Days

1. **Music:** What kind of music do you like? Have you created a playlist for this situation? If so, that's what you have to communicate to people and/or write down. See Resources section for more information.

2. **Flowers:** I knew a person in hospice recently who felt inundated with the amount of flowers she received. It really is true – you can have too many flowers. If you love flowers, then perhaps it will be fine to have plenty around while you are in your last days. If not, you need to make this clear, and what kind you love or hate. Bear in mind that some hospitals may not allow flowers.

3. **Atmosphere:** What kind of atmosphere do you prefer? Do you like aromatic smells? Do you prefer silence to music, conversation, background hums, radio? What's your take on candles or incense?

Remember to keep this information updated otherwise you might be hearing and smelling things from your past that you would rather not. The other thing to bear in mind here is that as the body becomes more and more frail, and releases its life, it may become more and more sensitive too.

"One really useful piece of advice that I used with my mother, and I would like to pass on to other people, is this: if you are with someone who is dying it's much better to put your hand underneath their hand, rather than putting your hand on top, because then they can take their hand away if they want to. If you put it underneath, they have the contact, but if they want to have their hand back they can just take it back; plus it is less pressure."

— Christina, England

"I do not like people touching my feet at all, so that's something I will add to my document; my sister knows for sure, but others do not."

— Janet, USA

Watch out for making assumptions; the more information you can give to your family and friends the better.

Saying Goodbye

A family member who died last year was quite clear that visitors were to stop coming to see him in the hospice as soon as they began to feel uncomfortable with the situation. This meant that some people did not have the 'I'm saying goodbye now' conversation. Alternatively, others feel that is very important. You can make a decision about this and write down what you want.

> "I visited a friend last year who was dying. I didn't know what I was going to say when I got there, but I just knew I had to say goodbye. In the end I said, 'This is just awful isn't it', and then 'I love you' and asked if we could pray together. Then I said 'I'll see you on the other side' and left. I think it's important to be able to come and say goodbye, or for the dying person to say they would like people to come and say goodbye."
>
> — Ruth, USA

Death Doulas or Soul Midwives

These are people who are trained specifically to sit with a dying person, often having been involved over the preceding few weeks or months. This can be useful if for whatever reason the family or friends don't want to, or can't be there, or there is no-one suitable. Some people prefer the anonymity of someone whom they know less well, preferring not to 'burden' their family. Others can't even imagine why one would have someone around who is not part of the family. It's just a personal choice. See Resource Section for more information.

CASE STORY: Diane

Diane, a Canadian participant on one of the *Before I Go* courses, created a letter to her family after one of the discussions during one of the modules in the course:

Dear Ones,
As I review my final arrangements, will, etc., I'm reminded that there is a whole lot of info I might provide to you about my last days. Unless I die suddenly there's no need to talk about it. The proverbial truck or the not-waking-up-in-the-morning scenario make logistics simple.

However, if I'm not lucky enough for that to be my finish, here are some things I would like to have happen in my 'last days.'

You've heard me say I would like to die at home, if possible. It seems like the 'system' is more amenable to paying for home care where feasible. So let a professional take care of my bodily needs. It's less embarrassing for all.

If home isn't the house on _____ , then someplace homelike. I'd like to be able to see outside so I can connect with the trees that are home to my spirit.

Please, no clergy of any kind. If you need that comfort for yourself, please do so in another location. I would like to have my dogs with me for the loving comfort they are and the amazing connection we have. I know that someone in my family will take care of them physically and bring them to me when possible.

If members of my family and/or my goddess group can be there in shifts I would like that. Tell all my friends to drop in to say goodbye if they can. Don't be frightened; how about a last big hug!

I would love to have a pampering environment. Buffered from outside noise, with chimes/nature sounds/soft new age music. Silence is ok too. Flowers of course... preferably as potted plants that people can take home later to plant.

My favourite smells are lavender and roses, candles burning would be cool. If I am in pain I would prefer to manage it with cannabis, which my son can advise on. I'd like to be me when I go, not morphia-woman. But, I prefer people not see me in pain, as I know it would hurt them more than me.

Hold my hand... with your hand under mine so I don't feel trapped. Keep your sense of humour. Death is unavoidable and the ultimate joke. I would like to have my wolf totem near where I can touch it occasionally.

Don't fear saying goodbye to me. You all know how much I love you, as I hope I've told you plenty in better times. Know that I am not fearful, and I will go through this dying experience with curiosity and peace. Love each other, unconditionally.

Love, Diane

Pets

If you have a pet or animal of some kind, you need to think about who would care for them in advance. Remember to imagine along the lines of 'If I had died yesterday, what would happen to _____?' Make sure you have someone in place who can take care of them. I mention this here because although in your last days you are still alive, you may not be in a situation where you can care for your beloved pet. For instance, if you are in hospital or a hospice, or even where a dog could visit, they may be too excitable for the situation, or too disturbed by it, to the extent that it is distressing for you to see them. Even if you are at home, you may not have the strength to have the pet in the room with you.

> "A married friend of mine died just before she could document for her life savings to go to her two children. Her husband didn't ask his late wife's children if they would like her beloved dog; instead he sent it to the dogs rescue home."
>
> — Patty, USA

An acquaintance who died at home a couple of years ago found the presence of her much loved cat very upsetting. The cat would scratch at the door, or interrupt her while sleeping and she wasn't able to do anything about it. It gave my friend more comfort knowing the cat was being looked after by a neighbour than it did to have him still in the house.

> "I'm a volunteer for a cat rescue organization. The number of times we get calls from family members or friends asking us to look after a dying relative's cat is enormous. Often the families don't know anything about the cats, and are at a loose end, which is why they ring us. Trying to sort through what the ill person would want can be really difficult for us, because we don't know and the family members don't know either. I can't tell you how heart-breaking it is sometimes; you know these animals are very loved by these people, but we have no idea what their wishes are."
>
> — Suzie, Canada

The moral of the story is: think about your pets in advance of anything being needed. Especially if your particular pet has got a lot of medical requirements, it all needs to be in a separate document, so make sure to attach a separate file with your plan, addressing your pets. Finally, there are organizations in most countries that help to take care of pets belonging to dying or deceased people. (See Resource Section.)

13

For Small Business Owners

· · · · · ·

"It's funny how most people love the dead,
once you're dead you're made for life."

— **JIMI HENDRIX**, American musician, 1942-1970

ATTUNEMENT: Take a pause. After reading this paragraph, just close your eyes and notice your breathing, and how your body feels. Pause, and reflect on your thoughts about your business in the event of your death.

When you run a business, whether you are a solo operator or head of an organization of hundreds, you have extra responsibilities. The premature death or even just incapacity of a business owner or staff member may result in a drop in sales, disrupted work patterns, and staff having to work extra or have time off. It can even result in the business being liquidated, sold to outside parties, or surviving family members having to become active in the business.

Grief at Work

In the UK, about 550,000 people die every year. If we assume a minimum of four people grieving for each one of those, that is over two million people being affected by those deaths. In fact, research has shown that at any one time, one in ten of us is in mourning. That is a lot of grief, and many people at work being affected. Companies have been slow to catch on about this, and not many have a bereavement policy. When they do, they often allow 1-5 days off work after a bereavement (depending on the nature of their relationship to you) and nothing at all for any other co-workers who may also be grieving.

Yet the effects of grief can show up in all kinds of ways; for instance, lower productivity levels, inefficiency overall, extra days off work. This is either because the grieving person cannot work, or because they are having to take care of the administrative after-effects of the deceased. Grief-related problems such as anxiety, stress due to family arguments over the deceased, or even physical illnesses are all commonplace, and often result in time off. If you are a business owner, it pays to learn about the effects of grief, how they play out, the effects on departments and teams, and what to do to counteract this. *Before I Go Solutions* ® provides products and programmes to help staff cope with the shock of bereavement and to lessen the effect on the overall business, the staff members, and individual departments. Visit the business section of **www.beforeigosolutions.com**

The Financial Impact of Your End of Life

Consider in advance whether the business would lose profits, be able to continue trading, and pay employees and suppliers if you or another key member died. Would loans to the bank still get paid? Who would be responsible for the signing of cheques or payment of salaries and wages? What happens if one necessary signatory, for any circumstance, is no longer available? Consider your own family and personal circumstances, and how your death would affect them (see later for more information on family-owned businesses). It is crucial to face up to the possibility of your own death while working, and have structures in place in case the worst happens. Also make sure you have the relevant insurance and that it is kept up to date.

> "My UK accountant admired me for being so organized when I said I was preparing in advance for when I was no longer here. Then he said, 'You need to make it clear that you wish our firm, rather than me personally in case of my own death or incapacity, to finalize your accounts and file any required tax returns.' I hadn't thought about tax returns!"
>
> — Kate, France

According to an Every Business Matters study in the UK, [19] 45% of UK business owners would expect their remaining fellow owners to buy their share of the business in the event of their death. But only 40% have actually taken out insurance cover to make sure funds are available for this purchase. Without this kind of insurance, others may find themselves having to fork out their own money to ensure the business continues, or risk it folding. Arranging insurance can help trading continue, and equally important gives staff, suppliers and customers the confidence that salaries can still be paid, and that there are enough funds for the business to trade through a difficult time. This is exactly what didn't happen in the next case study.

CASE STORY: Maria

"In 1996, together with my business partner, we set up a food importing business from the UK to Spain. We had our own supermarket in Benidorm, which was really successful and ended up with 20 employees between the supermarket, the van sales, warehouse and office staff. However, I became a vegetarian but was importing English sausage and bacon, and it just didn't feel right anymore. I spoke to my business partner and said I wanted to keep my money in the business, but I needed to do something else that really worked for me. He was in agreement with this. It was 2005 and we had just made a huge investment in buying a warehouse that was being built. We had both signed for a big mortgage as guarantors. I was ready to step out into a bright and sunny future, being supported by the income from the business. It felt like a smoothly oiled machine as the business was working really well. But none of us know what is going to happen, not really.

In October that year my partner went into hospital with unexplained pain, had an operation and never came round from it. He was 45. Nobody saw that coming – there had been no history of him having problems. It was a terrible shock for everyone at work, not to mention his widow and family. No-one coped well. He hadn't made a will – things would have been a lot easier if there had been one – as it was complicated because of being married previously with children from that marriage. Apart from all the emotional turmoil of losing someone very close to me, I now had a business that I didn't really want. Everything was up in the air. I had no idea where I stood legally, my partner's son with dependants was working in the business, and I had to sit in long meetings with my accountant and lawyers and work out what it was I was allowed to do, not allowed to do, and what I was compelled to do by Spanish law.

My partner was the one who ran the warehouse and went to the office every day. I had only gone to the office once a week. So my life completely changed. First thing I had to do was to decide whether to carry on, despite not wanting to. But I felt an obligation to the employees – several of them said how much they depended on their jobs; they had mortgages to pay, families to feed. On the other hand I felt insecure about finances. I had been receiving a good salary and the business was doing well. The obvious solution was to stay.

I found the hardest thing was dealing with the staff. My partner had been fabulous with people; he knew how to connect with them and to manage them really well, but I found it quite difficult. I thought they didn't like me, and of course we were all grieving for him and missing him terribly. I was up against this all the time. I first had to look at reorganizing. I had to replace what John had done – I quickly promoted someone into the position he had held. In my insecure thinking, I made rash decisions that didn't work out well in the long term. We had a lot of systems in place, but finding a replacement for the work that John did was the hardest thing. It was hard trusting people – I knew I could trust John 100%. But I never had that feeling again within anyone within the company. I had a constant underlying worry that I couldn't trust the people around me.

It was 2005 when John died, and profit margins had already started being impacted by new competition and the recession. So afterwards I took on a business coach. He could see the writing on the wall, but it took me a lot longer to see. I didn't want to be a failure. We were losing money so we needed to keep the supermarket but shut down the van sales in 2007 – I had to make a lot of people redundant. Very hard, and I didn't do it all at once. And then I had to do the same thing with the supermarket. In 2009, that closed, and I was left with a lot of debt, as was his wife – she inherited half the debt, and I had to take on the other half. Because there was no will, the family had no entitlement to what to do in the business until probate was sorted which took a long time. The three children and his widow all felt entitled. I was legally advised not to give them money and yet they wanted it. It was all very emotional.

Looking back now, I wish I had taken time to grieve myself. I set about firefighting, as there were so many different departments that all needed attention, but with hindsight, the most important thing was that I take care of myself. Even now in 2017 it is not all totally sorted out – but if there had been a will, this would all have been taken care of. The first thing I did as a result of all this was get a will for myself. The long term effects of not taking responsibility for the business as a separate entity is serious – it had effects on employees, me, his widow, his children – all were affected by him not having a will, and us not having discussed what would happen if one of us died. If we had done that, then we would probably both have had a will."

– Maria, Spain

Types of Business

Death affects different businesses in different ways, depending on the type of business that is being operated. However, read each of these sections, as what is in each of them may apply to how your particular company is set up and operates. Often known as succession or business continuity plans, your end of life plan for your business needs to include who will succeed you, and how that should happen, but there are numerous other details that need to be thought about too.

1. **Solo Professionals**

   Often, if you are self-employed and don't have anyone else working for you, or only contract work out, then it is easy to think you don't really have a business. However, if this is how you earn money, then you will have customers or clients. You have a responsibility to them, which, if you take care of it, will make life a lot easier for them after you have died. Your business may die when you die (most likely, unless you have set things up to ensure it continues), but your customers and clients are still very much alive.

   In the psychotherapeutic tradition, supervision of your work is required. This means that your supervisor will likely know about your clients, and could be an appropriate person to have contact details. If not them, then think carefully about who would contact your clients or customers if you die while you are still working. They would need to be provided with clear instructions and contact details so your clients are not left wondering what happened when you are not there for any appointment. This is particularly the case in cities, where it is quite possible your clients or customers will not know anyone else associated with you. In small communities, word gets round more easily about deaths in the village or town, and so they may hear this way, but is that the way you would want that to happen? Give this matter some thought, and have a system in place to deal with it. The above also applies if you have a partnership.

From an administrative point of view, state in your will (and elsewhere) exactly what you want done with your business assets and liabilities, if there are any. Take professional advice for this if you feel at all unsure.

2. Partnerships

Depending on the nature of the partnership agreement, your partnership will either dissolve upon one partner's death, or if it is a limited or limited liability partnership, then that is not necessarily the case. A written agreement is needed to detail what you wish to happen, and to set out how that might happen. For instance, a mutually agreeable purchase price, and a provision for an adjusted price if necessary, might be arranged in the case of death. Then the purchase could be funded by an insurance option paid for by the company. Make sure you know what is legally required in your country or state, and get advice if necessary.

3. Online Businesses

Many businesses these days are run entirely online, thus they have systems and structures to enable them to work effectively, and may not employ any people at all (rather just contract work out to other self-employed people or businesses). Even if yours only has a web presence, you still need to check that the systems will work smoothly if you or someone in a key position dies. Could the business continue on without you? How long will those systems continue on without any input from yourself? Who is responsible for managing what in your company? What do you have in place to take care of the online systems when a key person is no longer there – and particularly if they are no longer there all of a sudden? Have you considered the intellectual property you have and what to do about that? Will sales still be made, and money come in? Or have you underestimated the effect your presence has on your staff, your systems and your business in its totality?

4. **Businesses with Physical Premises**

   Much of the above applies here too, but if you also have premises of which you are in charge, who else has the keys, or the authority to have the keys? Who else knows how to open up, operate the alarm system, how to open the safe? Are there systems associated with the buildings that depend on you, or another key person, and what happens if you or that person is not there? Think this all through and develop systems and structures to take care of these eventualities.

5. **Corporation or Limited Company**

   The death of one of the shareholders in this kind of organization does not affect the company unless there is a written agreement to the contrary, because the company is an entirely separate entity to the shareholders. When a shareholder dies, his or her shares are distributed to the shareholder's heirs as personal property according to the law in your country or state, or as directed by the shareholder's will. However, it's not uncommon for an agreement to state that a company or corporation buy out a shareholder in the event of death. Checking your certificates of incorporation is important, to discover what is required to happen in the case of the death of a shareholder.

"I was director of a large company. A young apprentice was killed in a car accident, which affected everyone in the organization greatly. He had a small daughter and an ex-girlfriend; he had no will. We decided to close for the day of the funeral so everyone who wanted could attend, which was the right decision. I had to organize the payment of life insurance, pension etc., and to whom this should go, as the young man had not had a will or anything in place. In the end, I had to make the decision to whom the money should go to, and it was given to his parents. They bought a house with it, with the purpose of renting it out and providing an income for the daughter. It was a very difficult situation for all concerned."

— Margaret, England

6. **Family Businesses**

Death of a family member in a family business obviously means that both the family and the business itself will be reeling from the effects of your bereavement, or anyone else's for that matter. As you know, grief can swamp the ability to make rational or good decisions, can affect efficiency, and completely disrupt daily routines, so knowing how to cope best when death hits is doubly important.

"We had our very first family meeting on Sunday on the veranda with sandwiches which was terrific really. I said I was doing the *Before I Go* course and that we all are going to do this journey together, but I'm instigating it. I've been asking everyone to get things done. Our will was one of the things that came up, and is definitely a priority for us."

— Anita, England

It is poor business practice to deny one's own death, or that of other family members, and it is a lot easier to deal with the possible eventuality of it happening before it actually does happen. It is much better to insist that yourself and other family members face up to the unpalatable idea of one of you dying and ask yourself the question:

What does this person do, that, if they were no longer with us, would affect the business, and how would it do so?

Be detailed and specific in your answers. Consider each person in the family associated with the business, even just by marriage. For instance, the death of a partner's spouse may have just as detrimental an effect on the business, albeit in a different way, as if that person themselves had died.

Planning in Advance

Taking action with the following five tools will help you prevent the sometimes disastrous effects of a death. The ones you choose to operate will depend on the structure of your company and your intentions for it.

1. Grant a limited power of attorney to a key manager, so they will have the authority to make decisions and continue business operations in the event of you being incapable to do so, for any reason.

2. If your business has several executive level staff members, establish an advisory committee to act if a key decision maker cannot for any reason. Consider how you would want that committee to make decisions – it could be by consensus.

3. Create a document that would transfer your business interests to a trust on your death. The trust company would thus continue business operations on your behalf in the event of your death or incapacity.

4. Establish an employee stock ownership plan to make sure a buyer is available upon the owner's death.

5. Implement a buy/sell agreement if there are co-owners, key managers or other employees who might be interested in purchasing the company. A buy/sell agreement could be between shareholders, partners, or a key employee and a sole trader. The agreement would allow the surviving business owners, key employee or the business itself to purchase the interest of the deceased owner. Take specialist advice depending on your situation.

"Death and dying is particularly taboo in a family business because the belief tends to be that things will just carry on as they do, everyone knows what they're doing anyway, because nothing is written down, and there is no formula."

— Anita, England

14

Obstacles to Taking Action

· · · · · ·

"What the caterpillar calls the end of the world,
the master calls a butterfly."

— **RICHARD BACH**, American writer, b. 1936

ATTUNEMENT: Take a pause. After reading this paragraph, just close your eyes and notice your breathing, and how your body feels. Reflect on your thoughts about what obstacles might get in your way. Pay attention to what comes up instinctively about this, as these particular obstacles will almost certainly present themselves to you.

If you haven't already experienced something getting in the way of you attending to everything stated so far, then you are unusual! Our own end of life is such a challenging subject to deal with that obstacles, blocks and procrastination are entirely normal, even to be expected. There are such a lot of decisions to be made that it can feel quite overwhelming at times, with the result that it is only too easy to put things aside, thinking to come back to them later, and before you know it, months have gone by, or even more. One private client told me that she knew her will needed updating, but it had still been in her inbox for four years.

The main obstacle to making decisions about all end of life matters is that you are trying to decide what you want in a future that is unknown. Decisions about who you want around you when you die, about what you want in your Advance Directive, about who to have as an executor, not to mention all the others, are a huge challenge because you really do have to face up to the fact that you are not going to be around forever.

Here's seven of the more common obstacles and what to do about them.

OBSTACLE 1: Fear of Making a Commitment

When you write your wishes about anything down, it's really easy to think that means they are set in stone forever. This isn't necessarily a conscious thought, but it is one of the things that gets in the way of writing something down. When you put pen to paper, or complete your computer documentation, the putting it out of your head and down on paper or computer screen can seem very final. It does make it all seem more serious, or that it can't be changed. If you only tell someone your wishes, then you can delude yourself into thinking this means it will happen, but that is just not the case. Particularly so when you haven't made a proper will, or have a power of attorney or advance directive, I am sad to say you are indeed only deluding yourself.

If you recognize yourself in this last paragraph, then try saying this sentence out loud and notice how you feel afterwards:

'It's good enough for now, and safe enough to try.'

'Good enough for now' means that, given your circumstances right now, what you have stated will work. It means that if you died suddenly tomorrow, you could rest assured that your remains and your estate would be dealt with as you wanted. It means that if you knew that you had died yesterday, you would feel satisfied that your wishes were going to be carried out. What's more, others in your family, and your friends, would know that too, and generally speaking, this brings comfort and soothing at a time of distress.

'Safe enough to try' simply means that you have found things you would want to have happen at the end of your life that you feel happy with. It is safe enough to write these down, and see what it feels like. So now I invite you to go ahead, and try an experiment.

Select three of your end of life wishes, write them down and look at them. Notice how this feels; what sensations you feel in your body, and what your thoughts are about your wishes. If any of them don't feel safe enough to be written down in this way, then amend them so that they do. Remember the 'try' part – you are trying out this exercise to help you discover not only what you want but to enable you at some point to commit it to paper.

When a statement you make about your end of life wishes is good enough for now and safe enough to try, it means you have found a workable means of moving forward. It doesn't have to be perfect – in fact, it may never be perfect. The whole sentence means you can review your wishes in a year or two's time – in fact you can diarize that right now, to check up on what state your end of life plan is within two years, say. There is wiggle room, and where there is wiggle room, it makes commitment much easier, even if you never actually wiggle.

OBSTACLE 2: Fear of Getting It Wrong

Human beings often think there is a wrong and a right way to do things. The fact is, on this subject, there's only what feels right for you, right now. It may coincidentally be acceptable for a whole lot of other people, some in your family and some not, but that doesn't mean to say it's right or wrong per se. It's *your* feelings, thoughts, words, and decisions right now. Nobody else's. We know now from Obstacle 1 that these can change, and are meant to change as your circumstances change. At that point, the wording or documentation can be altered to reflect your circumstances at that time. So throw right and wrong out the window, and try out a decision instead.

OBSTACLE 3: Fear of Offending People

It's not uncommon for people to shy away from making a statement in writing because they imagine that those mentioned will be offended in some way. If you identify with this, then you are putting their feelings before yours. I don't mean to say that you shouldn't include their feelings, or work to find a compromise, but it is important to include yourself and your wishes in that decision too. If you find the thought of putting yourself first a challenge, then that is something to really reflect on. If you can't let yourself have what you really want in your end of life plan, then when can you? Perhaps you can talk to the relevant people; you might be amazed at what could happen.

"The fear of offending people – that kind of hit home with me partly because I have some pretty strong feelings I've developed over the last few years about cemeteries and burials. In many towns, cemeteries are literally running out of space. Locally, there have been some very heated discussions and Town Hall meetings about whether the land should be used to build a new high school for the next generation, or for burying us old people. So, frankly I've made a joke of it and when I talk to people I say I want to be buried as a tree. What I mean by this is that there are companies where you can have your ashes sent and they clean them up and then they put them in a little bio-degradable urn, and you go and bury yourself and you grow as a tree. Sometimes people ask what I mean, and I don't tell people that they shouldn't use up land or get buried; I just talk about coming back as a tree. So, I think it opens up conversations and the more we talk about it I think the more accepting of the kinds of things we will become."

– Diane, USA

OBSTACLE 4: Not Knowing What You Want

If you are the kind of person who finds it hard to even admit you have some desires or wishes, let alone state them, or write them down, then this will mean it is very difficult to know what you want. If this is the case, then it's likely happening in other areas of your life too, and therefore is a symptom of a much bigger picture and not in the remit of this book. However, sometimes not knowing what you want is just a manifestation of other thoughts and feelings, so check out the other obstacles, and be ruthlessly honest with yourself. Do you really not know what you want, or is there something else going on? Dig deeper and find out.

If you are the opposite type of character, and you want what you want and it doesn't matter about anyone else, then that is just the other side of the same coin. Both are reflections of a lack of self-esteem, and the challenge for both extremes is to find a balance – something that works for you, and also works for the relevant family members or friends. When you can find this balance, then the fear of getting it wrong, and of committing yourself to paper also more easily disappears.

OBSTACLE 5: Procrastinating

Procrastination is putting off something that needs to happen, but that you really don't want to do very much. It applies to almost everything in this Guide, and is one of the biggest obstacles to getting end of life matters taken care of. Just in case you think you're not a procrastinator, here's some of the ways it tends to show up:

- Your mind says things like:
  - 'OMG, I shouldn't be doing this'
  - 'I'll just do X and then I'll get to Y'
  - 'I really must get my _____ done'
- You have a nagging feeling that something is sapping your energy and you really ought to stop, slow down, work out what it is and then take care of it.
- You make a long list of things to do (even prioritized) and then regularly get distracted and do something else.

What is very common with procrastination is the extra layer of guilt we lay on ourselves when we know we should be doing something, but persist in not doing it. Recognize yourself? My antidote to this is:

> Take off the added layer of guilt, by admitting it is happening.
> Then make a conscious choice to procrastinate.

This means you give yourself full permission to do what you are doing, or want to do. It is no longer procrastination! Set a safe container for it by setting a boundary for 5 minutes, an hour, a day, a week, or however long you want. Then fully embrace what you are doing in that period of time and make sure you are enjoying yourself! The guilt has no place then, and the extra layer disappears.

Guilt can only thrive in an atmosphere of not-allowing. When what you are feeling guilty about is allowed fully, then guilt dissolves. Because this is such a huge thing for so many people, here are three more tips on coping with procrastination. See what takes your fancy to try out, or experiment with them all – you might be surprised at the results.

1. **Take baby steps.** Just like the amount of energy it takes to get a plane off the ground, so it can take quite a lot to get us going with anything. If you know you need to create your end of life plan, what would be a baby step that you could take today, to get you started?

2. **Tackle your end of life plan as a project.** Break it down into the tiniest of steps to enable the eventual end result of a completed plan, then not only are you more likely to actually complete the whole thing, but you will also get a sense of satisfaction and achievement at the end of each step.

3. **Do five minutes only.** Commit or attend to the thing you really don't want to do for five minutes. Not ten or twenty. Just five. This is like doing physical exercise when you haven't done any for ages; it's the getting started that is most difficult. You can choose to continue after five minutes if you really want to, but you will have succeeded if you simply do the five you committed to. Once that is done, then commit to another five at another point in time.

Get a free copy of 10 Ways to Avoid Procrastinating:
http://beforeigosolutions.com/guidepdf

OBSTACLE 6: Needing to Declutter but Being Overwhelmed By Stuff

Who has ever looked at all their stuff, realized it needed to be sorted, and given up just because it feels so overwhelming? It's a very common thing. Stuff is everything you have around you – some of it will be essential, some useful, some being kept for sentimental reasons, some just beautiful and gives you pleasure. There are many other reasons too, as those who like to keep a hold of their possessions will tell you. Not that this is necessarily a problem. It only becomes a problem when you literally can't move in your house anymore, or it becomes a health hazard, or interrupts your normal everyday life in some way, either practically, mentally and/or emotionally.

CASE STORY: Paul

My Dad died suddenly, and after the funeral, my brother and I went round to his house to start the process of clearing it. It was daunting, to say the least – there was so much. In fact, we had to arrange for a large skip. The thought of tossing years of possessions out was not good. A lot went to charity or thrift shops, but there was a lot more that was simply thrown in to the wet, dirty skip.

I am a natural hoarder so this took discipline and was difficult. Simply chucking out what had been part of my Father's life for over 50 years was harsh. Sorting personal items was a window into his life – notes, pictures of unknown people, odd electrical gadgets. He had five video senders. Why? There were things in the drawers that while useful in and of themselves, we had no use for. We had to harden our hearts; and the contents of the drawers went in the skip. I found lots of my Mum's belongings from when she had died 20 years previously, including letters, and a purse. Her work room had not been touched since then, so her industrial sewing machine was still there, with masses of dolls clothes, dressmaking fabric, and a huge plastic bag of zips – things that could have been given away to members of the family much earlier.

What did I learn out of this experience? If you want stuff to go to a good home, go somewhere useful, or be valued in any way because it has some significance, you have to organize that when you're alive. Make sure the story of it is known, as it is the story that adds the value. Because when you're dead no-one knows that story or history, and without that connection it will get burned or buried.

This process made me think about the two wooden fish in my own house, that I carved with my father when I was 10. My son will now inherit them, thereby creating a connection between the three generations of men in the family. I love that thought, of my son and Dad connecting through what I made with him.

The salient point is: make it is easy for those you leave behind. Get rid of stuff you do not need, label the important things; check with the family if they want them or not; send them to a good home before they just get dumped.

— Paul, Scotland

Stuff does just accumulate over a lifetime. Recently, my new partner was moving out of the family home in Glasgow, Scotland, to the town where I live. He and his late wife had lived there with their family for over 20 years. Clearing it out once the house was sold was a huge undertaking. He didn't find it easy, but with a date for the new owners to move in, he didn't have a choice. I helped him begin the process by taking one drawer from the kitchen. We emptied it out onto the sitting room floor, and then he allocated all the bits and bobs into three piles – rubbish, charity/thrift shop, and keep. The stuff that was kept went back in the drawer, ready to be packed into a box when the time for that came. The charity/thrift items were put in the back of the car, ready to be delivered. The rest went into the rubbish bin. It was quite an emotional eye-opener for him but was made easier with the presence of someone else.

"I remember when my parents cleared the family house out before they downsized; they didn't tell me that would mean I would lose my precious china pony collection from when I was ten. I didn't realize I still had it in their attic, but when I thought about it, I would have loved to have given those ponies to my niece. Too late, though."

— Mina, Northern Ireland

Someone is going to have to clear your house after you are no longer there. So who's it going to be – you, your family and friends, or a professional house clearer? Think about it; do you mind if all your possessions just get cleared out and you don't know where they will end up? If not, then you don't have a problem, and you need to state that, but if you do, then you need to start thinking about it now.

You may not think decluttering is a priority at all, especially if you are not terminally ill, or anywhere near death. However, as we know, it can happen at any time. So here's how to actually do it:

- Select one drawer in the house (or one small box, bookshelf or area).
- Get some empty bags or boxes, identify them for keeping, charity/thrift shop, rubbish/garbage, or for individual family members.
- Put all the contents of the drawer onto the floor or table.
- Pick up each item, be aware of its meaning and memories, ask yourself whether it still brings you joy, and then choose which category it comes into:
  - Thank it for what it has done for you or the family.
  - If you are keeping it, put it into that bag/box.
  - If not keeping, say goodbye, and place it in the relevant bag or box.
- Take bags to charity/thrift shop or to the recycling or landfill.
- Give yourself a high five or pat on the back.

You may have belongings that mean something to members of your family, like Mina's china ponies above. So when clearing, you might want to involve the family. You may want to pass on the story behind the ceramic vase that has always lived on your mantelpiece, or the heirloom that will be handed down to your grandchild, or the old photographs of family members from centuries ago. A story enables the beneficiaries to make a decision about what to do with them, even if you have not already taken care of that; and you may want to keep it if you are wanting to create your Living Legacy (see **www.beforeigosolutions.com**).

> "My older son came yesterday and picked up his photos – that's all the family photos away now. I didn't realize they were weighing so heavily on my mind. It has cleared my head for the rest of this stuff and it now just feels like I'm doing the last little odds and ends to make sure I have all my affairs in order."
>
> — Stephanie, Canada

OBSTACLE 7: Practical Lack of Support

It is not helpful in completing any of this that there are few formal systems around that allow recording of end of life wishes to be easily known by the health professionals, let alone our friends and family. One day I'm sure there will be these systems, as it seems so obvious that they are needed. For now, lack of systems doesn't make it easy.

There is also a lack of awareness amongst health professionals themselves. End of life care has not in the past been a large part of the teaching curriculum in the teaching hospitals and universities. As our ageing population grows, this I believe will change. In the meantime it is entirely possible that you will know more about various things (e.g.,an advance directive) than your doctor. Treat him or her kindly, explain its importance to you, and why you want to have one in place. The more educating we as the general public can do, the better. Alternatively, you may find your doctors are very well aware, and you will be in a position to learn from each other. However, in a surgery in England recently, one doctor was grateful to receive his patient's advance directive; but another doctor in the same practice incorrectly stated it was not a legal document. So until more education permeates its way through, double check what you are told.

OBSTACLE 8: Thinking You Are a Body Only

Is there more to who we are than a physical body? Depending on your views, your answer will be yes, no or anything in between. However, if your belief is that who you are is a body, and therefore when you die, that who you are also dies, it brings another level of complexity about facing up to the dying process. This is because you have to come to terms with the fact that there will be no more of you once you are dead. There's nothing wrong with that, of course, but many people who aren't yet clear about what their beliefs are, find facing up to the fact they will die a bit of a challenge. Believing that who you are is much more than the body can make it easier to face up to end of life, which actually means the end of the body only. If you're intrigued about this idea then read Chapter 7 and explore the Resources in that chapter to learn more.

15

After Death

· · · · · ·

"According to most studies, people's number one fear is public speaking. Does that sound right? Death is number two! This means to the average person, if you go to a funeral, you're better off in the casket than doing the eulogy."

— JERRY SEINFELD, American comedian and director, b. 1954

ATTUNEMENT: Take a pause. After reading this paragraph, just close your eyes and notice your breathing, and how your body feels. When you feel calm inside, reflect on your thoughts about what happens after death.

When people think about the practicalities of what will happen to them after death, they most commonly think about having a will and knowing whether they want to be buried or cremated. It's understandable, because anything else means really facing up to the fact that your life will end someday. But frankly, a will and knowing you want your body buried or cremated is not nearly enough; there are all sorts of other things to think about too.

Whatever your beliefs about a body, or what happens to you after you die, there will be a body left behind when whoever you think you are dies. Bodies do have to be disposed of, according to the laws of your country or state, although there doesn't have to be any kind of ritual saying goodbye, or ceremony of any kind. That is your and your family's choice, but if you don't make any decisions in advance, a funeral of some kind will almost definitely be arranged, because that is currently the norm in the Western world. This chapter deals with all matters to do with bodies and what can happen to them – information you need to know if you are to instruct others in what to do with your body.

Embalming

Wikipedia[20] states that embalming is the art and science of preserving human remains by treating them (in its modern form, with chemicals) to forestall decomposition. The intention is to keep them suitable for public display at a funeral, for religious reasons, or for medical and scientific purposes such as their use as anatomical specimens. In the late 1800s formaldehyde replaced the use of arsenic for embalming and is the foundation of what is currently used, which is now a mixture of formaldehyde, glutaraldehyde, ethanol, humectants and other wetting agents.

Embalming has not really taken off in the UK, but is much more considered normal in the USA. However, a body does not need to be embalmed. It is your choice. There is no right or wrong about it, unless according to your spiritual, religious, environmental or other beliefs you would be causing distress if you did or didn't ensure a body was embalmed. Let's take all judgments off this topic, so you can make an informed decision without guilt, embarrassment or shame attached.

Having said that, there are some circumstances when embalming is required legally (as in the case of repatriation), or if the body is going to be in a church or other place for any length of time. Sometimes in the case of a violent death, embalming and reconstruction might be the difference between a family seeing a loved one for the last time or not. Some people just do not want their body to be viewed and so embalming would not be necessary. Others want those left behind to have the choice to view or not, in which case thinking about how the body would look might be important. The thought of embalming to some may, at one extreme, seem to be about mutilating the body; while at the other end of the spectrum, to not embalm could cause considerable offence (to family members as well as funeral directors). You need to make a choice about this and if you do (or don't) want it to happen, indicate that in writing.

Organ Donation

This is almost always going to be possible only if you die in hospital. When someone dies at home, the length of time to get the relevant organs to the required place is prohibitive. However, as none of us know where we will die, this shouldn't stop you stating your wishes, just in case it is possible. Make sure they are written down and/or entered into the required organ donation website for your area.

This might be a case of priorities for you – if you'd rather die at home than donate your organs then that is how you will set things up. If you would like to have your organs taken care of then you need to set that up so people know you don't want to die at home, and that it is quite clear to all who need to know (including hospital staff) that you want whichever organs you have dictated to be saved.

Disposal of Bodies

Legally a body has to be disposed of, and in particular ways depending on the country in which you live, but there are options other than the most commonly known ways of burial or cremation. In 2016, a YouGov poll[21] in the UK showed that 58% of people want to be cremated when they die, with the vast majority (79%) then wanting their ashes to be scattered somewhere, with only 7% wanting them to be kept. In the USA the cremation rate has been steadily rising, with projection rates from the Cremation Association of North America[22] forecasting a rate of 54.3% in 2020, although rates vary considerably between states. In other countries in the world, it can be as low as less than 10%. It depends on factors such as cultural norms, religion, and beliefs. What is very important is to be able to make an informed choice about body disposal.

Options for Disposal of the Body

See Resources section for more information on all these options.

1. **Traditional Burial**
   This is the placing of a body in a hole in the ground (the grave) and covering it over. This usually takes place in a cemetery or burial ground, which may or may not be attached to a church or other place of worship. Often a stone with the name of the person who died is placed at the head of the plot, to mark the spot. This is what over the years has become sometimes very ritualized, and is often what is meant when people state they want a funeral. However, because of escalating costs of burials (amongst other reasons), the disposal of the body in this way is now sometimes separated from what was assumed to be simply a part of the whole ritual of a funeral.

2. **Green Burial**
   This is similar to the above in that the body is buried in the ground, but it is done so in an environmentally friendly way. Thus a green burial (also known as a woodland or natural burial) will focus on:

- Keeping things simple.
- Burial in a green burial site that has been designated as such. This means many plants and trees around, with emphasis on it being wildlife-friendly.
- No embalming (chemicals can be hazardous to the earth).
- Biodegradable coffin (cardboard, willow, bamboo, seagrass or sustainable wood of some kind; or a shroud of biodegradable material).
- No memorial stone (instead, a tree or bush may be planted on or nearby the grave).

3. **Home Burial, or DIY (Dig It Yourself)**
   Generally speaking, there are no laws against being buried in your garden, yard or land at your house. However, there are health and safety guidelines to follow, and in the UK you will need to notify the placement of the grave on the house deeds if you choose to sell. Check out the laws on this in your own state or country.

4. **Burial at Sea**
   This again will be governed by the laws within your country, so please make sure you follow those. In the UK there is guidance about how the coffin must be constructed and also how to conduct a burial at sea. If you want to be buried at sea, you definitely need to be organizing this well in advance.

5. **Cremation**
   This is the incinerating of the body at very high temperatures leaving a small amount of ash. Some countries and states have regulations as to where ashes can be scattered; make sure you have checked you will not be breaking the law when you state how you want your ashes disposed of. Traditionally, this method also includes a ceremony of some kind at the crematorium.

6. **Resomation (Water Cremation)**
   This is similar to cremation up until the point at which the body is no longer seen by the public. Instead of fire burning the coffin, this process uses a water-and-alkali-based method, known as alkaline hydrolysis, to rapidly reduce the body to ash and liquid.

The process is on average 3-4 hours long and once complete the pure white bone ash is returned to the family in an urn, just as happens with a flame cremation, the method by which most of us are more familiar. At the time of writing, this is a much less well-known option.

7. **Cryomation**
   This involves immersing a body in liquid nitrogen down to a temperature of -196 degrees, by which point it is very brittle. Then pressure is used to fragment the body into small particles, allowing for the removal of any surgical implants and other foreign material.

8. **Direct Cremation**
   This term applies when the cremating of the body is separated from the traditional method of cremation. The body will be cremated separately without the ceremony, which could happen at another place and/or time; or not at all – not everyone wants a ceremony to take place.

9. **Donating Your Body to Medical Science**
   The requests from a hospital or teaching establishment that is willing to take bodies will vary according to the area in which you live. It has to be set up in advance, and it does mean that the deceased's relatives and friends won't have a body with which to have a funeral or end of life celebration.

   This happened many years ago to a friend of the family who had donated her body for medical science. Her daughter arranged a memorial service without any coffin there, and it was fine. However, she didn't get the remains back for about two years, so it really is an option to be thought about in advance, and researched locally. Generally there is no age limit, nor is it necessarily a problem if the person had a terminal illness. You also need to have a Plan B in place, because the establishment may or may not take the body due to various reasons, including how many bodies they already have, or if there needed to be a post mortem. If this happens, you may still be able to leave your brain to a brain bank, or eyes to a specialist hospital etc.

"My father wanted to donate his body to science and he kept telling me it's all set up, but I didn't find the paperwork till about two weeks after he had died which was, by then, way too late."
— Michael, England

10. **DIY Body Care**

If you want your body to be taken care of by your family and friends, you ideally need to have discussed it beforehand. This is because there are many things to consider, much as there are with whoever takes care of the body. I highlight some of these here, as in the Western culture we are used to answering questions such as these, below, if an undertaker asks them, but not so used to considering the implications if our family or friends are going to be taking care of the body. Some of what you need to think about are:

- Whether you want family and friends to be able to view your body (and if so, when, where and for how long you would want that to be)
- Whether you would want your body washed and by whom
- What clothes (if any) you want to be dressed in
- What container (or shroud) to be used, and where to get it from
- How you would want your body to be transported to where it will be disposed of (check your local crematorium will accept bodies from those other than professional funeral directors)
- Which fit, able-bodied and emotionally willing people would be able to move the body around (within the house and to a vehicle)
- Who you would want to conduct any service, if you don't employ a professional celebrant or person of faith
- What vehicle would be used to transport the body (e.g., a coffin will usually fit in a normal sized estate car)

You can see why this might be overwhelming if it hasn't been discussed before, and it is the grieving family and friends who are trying to make the decisions. So do talk about it beforehand if this is an option you want to take up.

Often people are nervous about dealing with dead bodies, especially if they haven't seen one before, and in this day and age, that is not uncommon. However, if you know what to do, and feel confident about it, it's fine to have a body kept at home after the death. It used to be the norm, especially in the countryside, and not so long ago either.

If someone dies at home, you don't need to panic either, and call the doctor or the undertaker immediately (which may cost extra if it's 'out of hours'). People do wonder if a dead body will go stiff (rigor mortis) and be impossible to move. Actually, rigor mortis usually sets in after maybe a couple or hours or so at the earliest (or maybe even longer, up to 6 hours), and after a couple of days it wears off. The only thing you really need to ensure is that the body is kept cold. In a cool climate such as the north of Scotland this won't be a problem – open the windows and if necessary you can use ice-packs alongside the body. A funeral director told me they always recommend taping curtains to the walls of an open window, to avoid flies entering.

> "I remember as a child living in the country that it was normal for death to be at home, especially if someone died at home, to be just kept there, kept cool, dressed, and washed in a particular way (if they needed to be washed), and then allow the family and friends in to say goodbye. The undertaker was sometimes contacted to take the body away for the funeral itself, but even that was sometimes done by ourselves in the back of a van."
>
> — Kate, Scotland

However, in the middle of summer, or a warmer climate than the north of Scotland, an ice-pack probably isn't going to do a very good job for much longer than 24-48 hours after death. An air conditioning unit may work better. If using a funeral director, you may be asked to bring the body to the mortuary to keep it cool most efficiently, once everyone has seen the body. The person can then go home one or two days before the funeral. As always, check the requirements in your locality. Different areas within countries or states sometimes have local regulations or methods that you will need to abide by.

Do not let any of this kind of complexity put you off having a DIY disposal and funeral, if that is what you want to have happen. They absolutely can be done by your family and/or friends, and you can find more information about DIY funerals in different countries in the Resource section.

Funerals

The ritual acknowledgement of the ending of a life in Western society has traditionally been the funeral, which includes the disposal of the body either by burial or cremation. Nowadays, increasingly, and especially as costs for funerals have risen dramatically, more and more people are beginning to dictate how they want their funeral to be conducted, by thinking about it in advance. This includes having the body disposed of separately to any ceremony of farewell, as in direct cremation.

Funeral, Memorial, or End of Life Celebration?

It's easy to get muddled up between the terms 'funeral' and 'memorial' in particular. They are both end of life celebrations, arguably, but we don't or haven't been thinking of them like that until fairly recently. Often, we assume a funeral is what is done when the person has just died, and the memorial something done, much later on, to remember them by. In fact, a funeral refers to the ritual that occurs when there is the presence of a body. If there is no body, for whatever reason, then the occasion is known as a memorial. That's why there can be a funeral, and then even very soon afterwards, a memorial. The term end of life celebration may or may not include a body, and by the use of the word 'celebration' suggests an occasion less sombre than is often associated with funerals. The formality of black clothes, Victorian hearses and black horses with plumes are not always wanted these days, and this is perhaps why the term 'end of life celebration' has become more common.

Whatever occasion you decide you want, stating the music you desire or where you want the service to be held just touches the surface of what actually needs to be organized. When planning a wedding or other major life event, we spend months doing it. Why not with the end of life ceremonies? It's because our society prefers generally to ignore that death is going to happen, so nothing is planned in advance, and instead it's all left up to those who are grieving, not best placed to make decisions, and certainly not in a position to make sensible financial decisions. So I strongly encourage you to consider some of the points below. If you really want to bring yourself and your families peace of mind and relief, then being willing to think in depth about what happens after the death of your body is essential. There is so much more that can really help if you are willing to look at the fact that your life will, one day, come to an end.

"My mother and I had a discussion around what to go in her coffin; she wanted to be wearing her favourite dress. She also wanted a recording made by the local choral society that she sang with for many years, a blanket she had knitted, her Franciscan Tau cross, and a printout of her memories I had managed to type up while she could still read it. She also had a photo of her wedding day, an embroidered coaster my brother had made for her when he was about eight, one of her favourite scarves and a miniature of whisky! So, gifts from both her children, and things that represented who she was, and it felt a very loving and caring task to do for her, and a very powerful experience for me."

– Christina, England

The questions below are just a few from a free PDF you can access here: *25 Important Questions to Ask When Planning Your Funeral.* **www.before igosolutions.com/guidepdf**

- Do you want a funeral at all? (It's not essential)
- How do you want your body to be transported?
- What do you want your body dressed in?
- Who do you want to conduct any funeral service?
- What readings do you want in the service?
- What do you want people to do afterwards?
- Do you want an obituary and/or eulogy?

"My mother in law died, with a will, but no other instructions. I didn't know her well enough to know what she would have liked in the funeral service. I really wish she had left instructions about this; I would have loved to have carried out her wishes".

— Petra, USA

Undertaker or DIY?

Once you've decided how you want the body disposed of the next matter is whether or not to employ the services of an undertaker. Yes, you read it right – you do not need to have an undertaker or funeral director. This is a choice you can make, and neither is right or wrong.

The vast majority of people in the UK use a funeral director and what's more, the first funeral director that they contact. In fact, figures in the Royal

London National Funeral Cost Index 2017 show that only 6% obtained quotes from more than one funeral director. It's easy to understand why this figure is so low given relatives are in shock, grieving and perhaps find it distasteful to think about money at this time. However, given that the costs of these services vary enormously, with a difference at the time of writing of nearly £2,500 (over $3000US) between the highest charge and the lowest, it is obviously a good idea to think about this in advance. In order to be able to do this, you have to admit you are going to die, and do your research beforehand.

Undertakers (aka Funeral Directors)

It may be that you cannot conceive of all the things necessary in a funeral or end of life celebration without the professional know-how of a funeral director. That is absolutely fine. If you decide you want one, then (by planning in advance) you can choose someone whom you like, and with whom you can discuss what you want. It will all be recorded, and neither you nor your family will need to be concerned again. Your family or friends can simply call them up when the time comes and let them know they have a dead body in the house. You can also use them for all the services they provide or just some.

Remember, there is no right or wrong here, it is simply down to preference. (This is why it is important to be able to have end of life conversations with your nearest and dearest though – because otherwise they may very well be left with a list of instructions in your plan that prove a challenge to carry out. This happened with a friend of mine who died unexpectedly this year. She had completed her plan, but not discussed it with anyone. Her executor and friends really wanted to carry out her wishes, but in several ways this proved quite a challenge, and would have been made easier if she had thought it all through beforehand with at least one other person.)

Never underestimate the power of the wishes you have for your body. Those left behind will, generally speaking, find comfort in being able to give you what you said you wanted, and so will do their utmost to ensure that happens, which, at a time when they are already stressed by grieving, may prove to be quite difficult.

So it really is best that everyone knows beforehand your wishes, it has all been discussed, and there are no surprises afterwards for anyone, nor any reasons for arguments.

What a Funeral Director Can Do

Some of the things a funeral director can offer are: arrange the funeral with the crematorium or other place as designated; offer and drive the hearse and other cars, if you are having them; arrange the purchase of a coffin or shroud, arrange flowers, and transportation of the body. They can also wash and dress a body with or without the family present, arrange services in a church or anywhere other than a crematorium or cemetery chapel (e.g., a garden or woodland).

They will also be professional bearers of the coffin, although many family members like to do this themselves, if allowed to by the crematorium or burial site. They will collect someone from a hospital and keep them in their mortuary. (This is what happened to my husband.) Sometimes, a family will have a coffin delivered, the body is placed in it by the FD's, then the family comes to collect the coffin and off they go, without any more input from the FD's.

Protocol at Funerals

Depending on what the deceased wanted, what those organizing the funeral want, and your religious and/or cultural beliefs, nowadays anything can happen. These days, wearing black is not necessarily what happens, so if you are going to a funeral it's a good idea to find out what is the dress code. When my stepdaughter died, she had specified she wanted people to wear bright colours. However, I noticed as I was packing to go to England that I felt slightly nervous about this, hoping I wouldn't be the only one turning up in a bright colour. (I wasn't.)

CASE STORY: Don

"Don had been diagnosed with terminal cancer out of the blue, being told that he only had a few months to live. This was a huge shock to him and his wife Barbara, neither of them having had cause to suspect anything so serious. While he was still relatively well, he and Barbara asked for a Peace Prayer Ceremony to be held in their beautiful garden. It was a cloudy but dry day, and one by one, we took it in turns to present one of the 195 flags, representing each country in the world, saying 'May peace be in ....' An hour of peace songs two weeks later in the same garden was also planned. Sadly, Don died before this event, but made it known that he wanted it to go ahead anyway.

Don had also wanted to take care of his funeral himself. Together, he, Barbara and his son Mike organized a white cardboard coffin, placed in the summerhouse in the garden. They made sure there was easy access to paints, colouring pens and other materials for his family and friends to decorate. Don wanted everyone to wear colourful clothes, knew exactly what music he wanted, and where the funeral and end of life celebration were to be.

On attending the funeral, held in Newbold House, the local retreat centre where he and Barbara had been married, I was touched to see people standing around the coffin, which by now was fully decorated with beautiful artwork. Some were taking photographs. Something that is so often a cause of distress had become an object of great beauty. The service was held by an inter-faith celebrant, someone who enables the creation of something that particularly suits the individual who has died. This is made easier when someone is planning their own funeral beforehand. Don knew he wanted his daughter to read out the story of Burglar Bill, which he used to read to her in bed at night when she was little. He also wanted a passage from Wind in the Willows read out by his friend Marcus, who had spent many hours reading to him in the last weeks and days of Don's life. A poem written by friend John was read out by him. A simple shamanic ritual was conducted by another of his daughters. It was a service full of emotion – smiles, tears, poignancy. I have never laughed so much at a funeral – nor have I ever known people to applaud, which they did at the end of Burglar Bill. It was a beautiful example of a creation by the one person who could not be there in an alive body, and gave all those there permission to think about what they might like when their time comes."

— Jane, Scotland

Don's funeral emphasized this – the ritual ending of your life really *is* your choice. It can be the way you really want it to be, if you are willing, as he was, to face up to the fact it is going to happen. To take charge, to invite others to support you in its creation, and to die knowing that you were the instigator of an event where you will be the star of the show, even while not being there in body, can be wonderful, although not for everyone, by any means. However, for too long now people have been bid goodbye in a church where they had no associations; with a service conducted by someone who did not know them when they were alive; or with a meaningless ritual, given who they were in life. It no longer has to be this way.

Funeral Costs

In the UK in 2017, the average cost of a funeral was approximately £3800, with this doubling in London and some other major cities. In the USA, it was about $7000. In Australia, about AU$7000. The total will depend on how many of the optional add-ons are wanted – but many people don't realize that flowers, a headstone, removal of the body, celebrant or clergy fees, organist, hearse, extra cars and so on are not actually needed.

When the undertaker told me how much it was going to cost for Philip's body to be taken care of I burst into tears, and shouted at him, saying, 'I don't want to pay that sort of money for something I never wanted to have happen!' He just sat there and didn't say anything. Afterwards I discovered that the £2000 he had quoted was in fact relatively cheap. However, just after a death is not a good time to discover this kind of information – another reason to get this taken care of in advance, by buying funeral insurance, saving in a separate account designated for that purpose, or educating yourself about what components of a funeral are essential to you and what are not.

Conducting the Funeral or Other Ceremony

Should you choose to have a funeral, memorial, end of life celebration or other ceremony, it needs to be organized (which is why a document stating your wishes makes it so much easier on those doing the organizing). A funeral director may help with this, if you wish; alternatively, you can ask someone else to conduct proceedings. You may have one person for the actual funeral itself, and another for a memorial or other celebration of life. Whoever you ask, they will need to be in liaison with the funeral director/celebrant (if appointed) and family/friends for administrative arrangements.

In the UK, when many belonged to a church or religious community of some kind, the leader of that church or community would conduct the funeral for one of their followers, and traditionally everyone would retire to the family home for refreshments afterwards. He (in those days, it would most likely have been he) would almost definitely have known the person who had died. The deceased would have been considered part of the faith family, and it made sense for it to happen like this. If you are religious or spiritual, you may well want your vicar, rabbi, priest, imam, or leader of your local faith group to hold the funeral for you. If so, that needs to be communicated as well as written down in your plan. Otherwise people left behind might make incorrect assumptions, or disagree.

Celebrants

Anyone can lead a funeral, memorial or end of life ceremony; it doesn't have to be an 'official' – it could be a family member or friend. However, there are many different celebrants, religious leaders or officiants who can help, and will explain and plan the ceremony with you. They will describe what is involved in creating a ceremony and then plan it with you, taking into account the wishes of those who have died (if there are any). While a religious leader may have a protocol to follow, many celebrants will encourage your involvement in terms of understanding the essence of your loved one. They will help you select readings, poems, music, hymns, prayers, offerings and any other tributes you wish to make, or have made. Thus it becomes a very personal ceremony, with as much or as little of your own involvement as is agreed.

There are different types of trained and authorized celebrants, and it is common for people to be confused about this, thinking that the only alternative to a traditional funeral in a church or place of worship is a humanist celebrant. However, they are not the only option, and outlined below are some of what is available.

Civil Celebrants

These are people authorized to carry out a funeral in a dignified and culturally acceptable manner for those who, for whatever reason, do not want a religious ceremony. There are several different kinds of civil celebrants, although all believe the ceremony should be personal to who died and very much relevant to their life. That may seem obvious, but is another reason why you may want to state your ceremony wishes – assumptions are easily made at this point if those left behind do not know your wishes.

Faith and Belief Celebrants

This includes humanist, pagan, independent, interfaith and others. They differ in various ways; for example, humanist celebrants tend not to believe in religion and therefore would be unlikely to use prayers, hymns, poems or anything mentioning a religion of any kind. Humanists don't generally believe in any kind of afterlife either; however, this is an ever-growing and changing field, so check in your country or state as to what your local humanist's beliefs are.

An interfaith celebrant or minister embraces all faiths, and none, and will offer a service that centres around or includes elements of different faiths if you would like that, or not as you prefer. Hence a non-religious but spiritual person might choose elements from Buddhism, Christianity and Shamanism, or nothing at all, depending on their beliefs and values. Essentially an interfaith minister will respect and honour all faiths and traditions, and will work with you to create a service that is very personal to you in this respect.

Eulogy

The eulogy is a speech given at a funeral or other ceremony commemorating and celebrating the life of the person who has died. It is often given by the person conducting the funeral, but it can also be a family member, family friend, or another appointed person. You can also write this in advance yourself, and appoint someone to read it out. Again, simply make it clear what you want to have happen.

Obituary

This is the notice of death that traditionally was (and still often is) inserted in newspapers to inform readers as to the death. It may be an article outlining the person's life as well as information about the details of any funeral or other gathering that will take place. You may write it yourself in advance, appoint someone to write it for you, or leave it up to those left behind to make the decision. More informally nowadays, friends and acquaintances often hear about a death via Facebook or other social media; see Chapter 16 for more on the impact of death on your digital life. However, if you want to make sure notice of your death reaches as wide an audience as possible, a formal death notice in the obituary columns of your local (or national) newspaper is still very effective.

16

Your Digital Life - Passwords, Privacy, and Pragmatism

• • • • • •

*"How can the dead be truly dead when they still live
in the souls of those who are left behind?"*

— **CARSON MCCULLERS**, American novelist, 1917-1967

ATTUNEMENT: Take a pause. After reading this paragraph, just close your eyes and once again, notice your breathing, and how your body feels. When you begin to feel calm inside, reflect on your thoughts about what your digital life looks like.

Share Medium Viral WhatsApp Livestream User Online Blockchain PC Netiquette Virtual Reality IoT Message Digital Etsy Legacy Amazon Swipe Micro Netflix Content Texting PayPal Clickbait Vimeo Gmail Bitcoin Hashtag Mobile Reddit Post OS Facebook Social Pinterest Data Android Media Keywords Influencer eBay Flickr Twitter WWW Tweet Instagram SMS UGC Status Offline Google Kindle Chat Skype Buzzfeed iMac SEO Ai Password LinkedIn Behance Friends Apps

This now deserves a whole section to itself, as our lives these days are so often about our online presence. Even if you aren't on social media of any kind, most people have online bank accounts, utility bills, or other administration online. If you don't have an online presence of any kind, then you can skip this section.

It's easy to underestimate the amount of electronic information that is stored on computers or on the web. Upon your death, this information is still there, and needs to be dealt with. A recent Co-operative Bank survey[23] in the UK found that while almost all bank customers now have access to their accounts online, 75% have not made any arrangements for someone else to know the details of those bank accounts. Out of more than 2,000 adults surveyed, 78% of those trying to manage a deceased person's online bank accounts, utility, shopping and social media accounts were experiencing problems. But only 16% of people had said they wanted their next of kin or anyone else to have access to their social media accounts, let alone any other type of account. This is an area of law that is not clear. While it can be considered an offence in USA to use another's password even with their permission, this is clearly not what we are talking about here.

So what to do? It is understandable that while you are still alive, you don't want anyone else to have access to any of your private information, and yet what happens when you die, and especially if that death occurs suddenly? A way round this has to be found. Many would think it was safe to include this information in a will, but because a will may not be accessible until some time after the death this is not practical. Even more importantly, a will is a public document, so whatever you do, do not put this kind of information in your will.

Examples Of Digital Assets		
Artwork	Music	Text Messages
Emails	Financial	Virtual Currency
Games	Photos	Websites
Maps	Social Media	Work Product
Money	Software	Publications
Movies	Professional	Health/Medical

Passwords

If you are online a lot, you may want to consider using a password manager to securely store your passwords. (See Resources.) This means you (and anyone else you choose) only has to remember one password in order to access all of your others. However, many people don't trust this kind of system, and even if you do, it is wise to have a paper backup somewhere, if you can keep it up to date. This whole question brings up the issue of who to trust, as was mentioned before.

Ultimately, you can't know for sure whether or not whom you trust will carry out your wishes. That's what trust is about – feeling you know the person well enough to believe they will do so, or that in their professional standing they will be compelled to do so. So whether you decide to have an online password manager, a paper document or another system for recording your passwords, make sure that at least one other person knows your system for managing these. Without it, if you are not around, life is made much more difficult for those left behind.

> "I have what I call a digital executor, someone who is responsible for my online accounts but doesn't have responsibility for my will, financial power of attorney or advance care directive."
>
> – Selina, Australia

Social Media Accounts

It can be quite upsetting to discover a person's social media profile when you know they have died; and yet, some people find solace in it. Increasingly, social media is becoming an accepted way to announce someone's death – and yet there are many who discover the death of a colleague or distant friend from their Facebook newsfeed or on Twitter. Not the most sensitive way by any means.

It wasn't so long ago that, because of privacy laws, it was quite a challenge to close down an account. However, Google [24] now have an Inactive Account Manager which deals with this, and Facebook have their system to Deactivate, Delete and Memorialize [25] your account, including an opportunity to name a Legacy Contact.

Other internet-based organizations, including social media companies, will also have their own ways of dealing with this, which will no doubt change with time and experience. However, at the time of writing, many of them invite you to set things up before you die. Hence the importance of being willing to face up to the one thing that no-one wants to admit will happen to them.

Your Digital Legacy Plan

1. Create Your List

Make a note of all your digital assets and how to access them all.

- Social media (Facebook, Twitter, Instagram and any others)
- Email accounts
- Bank accounts
- Financial sites
- Photo sharing sites (Picasa, Flickr, etc.)
- Ebay
- Amazon
- Other shopping sites
- Travel sites/frequent flier sites
- Professional membership sites
- File sharing sites (Google Docs, Dropbox, etc.)
- Media sites (You Tube, Netflix, etc.)
- Online cloud backup systems
- Medical or health accounts
- Online publications
- Spreadsheet files
- Document files
- Own website or blog
- Gaming accounts

2. Appoint a Person

Appoint a person to take care of this; someone who is tech-savvy preferably. Maybe more than one, for different things.

3. Tell Them What To Do

Leave specific instructions as to how you want your accounts handled; e.g., a Facebook memorial page? Where do any PayPal funds go? Who has access to your online photos?

4. Keep in a Safe Place

Decide how you will keep this information. In an online service that stores passwords, or in another secure environment? Keep paper backups.

5. Keep It Up To Date

Your accounts, passwords, etc. will change regularly. So keep your Digital Legacy Plan up to date. One way to do this is to review it every year, in your birthday week.

Alternatively, you may want your online presence to stay 'live' in the form of an online avatar, a service that is about to be launched in America, or for posts you have written to be made after your death. Whatever it is, to be in control of what happens, you need to think about it now and particularly so if you are interested in this recent development of an online avatar after you have died. These are created while you're still alive, with the purpose of being able to communicate with your loved ones after you have gone. Whether this will take off or not remains to be seen – it still requires people to face up to the fact that they are going to die, well before the event actually happens.

> "We are now in a social media world and people don't think about the fact of how awful it might be to have their account still open after they have gone. We managed to close my mum's Facebook down because we didn't want to be going on there and seeing her, or to have her friends ringing us and saying, 'why isn't your mum responding? Oh I'm sorry, I forgot to say she was dead.' It's really the practical nature of getting everything done and dusted so it's out of the way, and that's why I'm doing this work now."
>
> — Elizabeth, England

If you think about the information stored online about you as your electronic assets, then it's easy to understand that it needs to be addressed in a similar way to which you would address your tangible assets such as your property, vehicles and other possessions. Follow this diagram to ensure you have all your digital life taken care of and consider appointing a 'digital executor' who is well-versed in the online world to take care of this aspect of your affairs.

17

Keeping It All Up to Date

• • • • •

*"I'm not afraid of death because I don't believe in it.
It's just getting out of one car and into another."*

— JOHN LENNON, British singer/songwriter, 1940-1980

ATTUNEMENT: Take a pause. After reading this paragraph, just close your eyes and notice your b reathing, and how your body feels. Notice especially any thoughts of resistance you have about keeping things up to date. No need to engage with them; simply acknowledge them and focus on your breathing and how your body feels.

Once you've done everything laid out in these chapters, you can justifiably polish your lapel, walk tall and feel proud. But as the saying goes, 'pride comes before a fall' and there is still another step to take. You need to keep it all up to date. Well, you don't *need* to, but if you don't review (and if necessary revise) regularly, then you risk things happening that are no longer appropriate, or not what you would wish.

For example, you risk someone who was named in your documentation having died, and if there was no other named person, then by default your estate would be dealt with by the authorities.

> "Set yourself up to do a full review of your *Before I Go* package, every few years. Because there's all kinds of things that can change, but one of the most important things is, have any of these people that you've designated died in the meantime? I think it's such a shame if your wishes actually don't get carried out, and your effects are left to those whom you would rather not have left them to. What a waste!"
>
> — Fergus, Scotland

When to Make Amendments

Your plans (and especially your will) need to be reviewed and amended whenever there is a change in circumstances in your life – and/or every few years. Here's some of the situations that will require you checking your wishes are to stay the same, or to be amended.

9 Reasons to Review Your End of Life Plan

1. **Marriage (and Not Just Yours)**
   If you get married, then you will most likely want to, at the very least, amend your will in some way, or at least revisit it. You don't want to be in the situation I heard about recently when a colleague's brother had died suddenly. He had not updated his will, and yet there was one from 15 years previously which was still valid. This meant his estate was divided according to his wishes laid out at that time. Previously he had been married to someone who already had two children from her first marriage. Since then he had divorced, and remarried. The terms of the will resulted in his ex-wife and her children inheriting everything. As you can imagine, this did not sit very well with the new family. So on your wedding planner list must go 'attend to will'.
   It could be as simple as making an amendment to whom you leave everything, or buying a life insurance policy, but it does need to be done. If you did die suddenly, remember your money does not necessarily and automatically go to your spouse. Or what if you don't want it all to go to them? So take charge now, and get it done.
   With other marriages in the family, it's also worthwhile reviewing your legal documentation when the ceremony happens. What about if your daughter gets married to someone you really detest? Do you still want your inheritance to go to them? To avoid this kind of thing, you can use the word 'marriage' as a signal that means 'check my will'.

2. **Separation and Divorce**
   It seems a shame to be writing about this so soon after the previous paragraph on marriage, but the fact is, splitting up, separating and divorce do happen, a lot. So better to take care of the financial administration in a wise manner before it is really needed.

Once again, use this event as a signal to address your will. It might be fine to erase your ex-spouse or civil partner from your will, but you may still choose to leave some money to your former partner – or you may be forced to as part of a court settlement or for child care.

When divorce happens, it's not just your will that needs to be amended. There are other sections in your plan that will need to be changed, for instance, who knows your passwords; your power of attorney and/or health care proxy; your advance directive information, and any emergency contacts. If you've designated people in any insurance policies or other documents, these may need to be changed too.

3. **Birth of a Baby or Adoption**
   Everything changes when a baby comes along, not to mention what you need to do regarding your end of life plans. Most importantly, you must name a guardian in your will to take care of your child, should you not be there for any reason. Include them also as a beneficiary in your will. If you already have children, and have not attended to this, then include them too, plus if you have adopted a child.

   As the children grow up, regularly review that you are distributing your estate in the way you want to. The main point of all this is to lessen the likelihood of battles between siblings after you have gone. It is amazing how many siblings, who have always got on before, become different people after their parents have died, and the issue of inheritance raises its head. To prevent arguments and rifts, keep your will up to date and don't let your death be a reason for a war between your children.

4. **The Death of a Named Person**
   If anyone whom you have named in your documentation dies before you, such as your executor, your power of attorney, proxy or health care agent, or any other person you have named in any capacity, then you need to choose a new person(s) or make sure the alternative people designated know they are now fulfilling that role. If the guardian you have appointed to your child or special needs adult dies, the same needs to happen. In some cases, when

the designated person has simply moved away, this will require a
review and possible new person appointed.

5. **If You're Seriously Ill**
   If you've been diagnosed with a life-threatening condition,
   then you are faced with the reality of your own mortality, fair
   and square. This is a perfect time (albeit uncomfortable) to get
   your act together regarding keeping your documentation up to
   date. Yes, it might be a challenge, now that your death really is a
   possibility sooner than later. However, take heart from this book,
   which originated simply because my husband was willing to do
   just that. Remember we benefitted greatly from that conversation,
   discovering an intimacy and connectedness that one wouldn't
   normally associate with facing up to death.

6. **A Move to Another Country**
   Especially for legal documents, this is a time to double check
   what is still valid in the new country or state, and make any
   necessary amendments. It may also be a time to review named
   people in your other documentation, in case travel time makes it
   impractical for them to carry out the designated role.

7. **New Laws**
   If laws in your country or state change, then definitely check in
   with a financial advisor and/or lawyer to see how they affect your
   plan. If you move countries, find out if the existing documents
   you have are still legal in that country. This includes if you are
   moving within the UK. The likelihood is that some at least may
   not be, in which case you can get the right ones in place. You
   don't want to be feeling good about having an Advance Directive
   in place only for your family to realize too late that it is not valid
   because it was created in a different country.

8. **Increase (or Decrease) in Financial Situation or Estate
   of Any Kind**
   A big salary increase, sudden windfall, or an inheritance will
   mean a hike in your bank account. With a large amount of money
   comes extra responsibilities. This is when visiting a financial

advisor is essential. Don't put it off, otherwise you or your family will find yourselves in a muddle that could easily have been taken care of well in advance. The same applies when you purchase an expensive asset such as a house, business or vehicles, or if you receive unexpected income from a business investment. A bigger estate in general may lead to more people fighting over it, but you can nip any possible disputes in the bud if you act now. Finally, if the nature of your property changes significantly, this also needs to be reviewed.

9. **Wanting to Change the Allocation of Gifts or Beneficiaries in Your Will**
   If the person to whom you have left a gift dies, or you change your mind about leaving them something, or the amount of money, then your will needs to be amended. Likewise, if you want to change, add or omit a current beneficiary.

Conclusion

• • • • • •

It's all very well reading this book, and becoming more informed, but the real purpose of it is to help you actually create your end of life plan. In order to do that, you need to make a commitment, take it step by step, and keep on keeping on until you are at a point where you can say, 'Yes, it's done!' – and then treat yourself to a celebratory marking of the occasion. It really deserves it!

It can be quite a challenge, and that's why I encourage you to do it with other people, making it a joint project, so to speak. You're all working on the same thing, and yet it is quite individual. That is what the online and offline groups offer – an opportunity to discuss your questions, hear from others' experiences, become clear in your own mind, talk with your family and friends – and then put your words down on paper.

This is why it is a process and needs therefore to be taken step by step. Once it is done, you have the process of regular reviewing.

To help you get started, keep going, and get the most out of this, there are several actions you can now take:

- Join the *Before I Go* mailing list, where you will receive the most up-to-date information, and useful, relevant articles. **www.beforeigosolutions.com**

- Take the free quiz and find out how well prepared you are or not! **www.beforeigosolutions.com/bigquiz**

- Join the *Before I Go* Facebook group: **https://www.facebook.com/groups/beforeIgo/**

- Get the *Before I Go Workbook*: **www.beforeigosolutions.com/workbook**

- Join one of the *Before I Go* groups – some online, some offline. **www.beforeigosolutions.com**

Even if you don't join one of the organized groups, get your friends and family together and make getting your end of life plans done a family project. Remember this quote by David Allen, author of *Getting Things Done – The Art of Stress-Free Productivity*:

> "I am rather like a mosquito in a nudist camp; I know what I want to do, but I don't know where to begin."

And then remember Mark Twain's famous saying:

> "The secret of getting ahead is getting started. The secret of getting started is breaking your complex overwhelming tasks into small, manageable tasks, and then starting on the first one."

So I encourage you to identify the small, bite-sized chunk you will take as a result of coming this far in the book, remember to enjoy yourself while doing it, and keep taking those small chunks until you have completed that task. Then go and celebrate!

Resources

• • • • • •

Free PDF downloads mentioned in this Guide all available from:
www.beforeigosolutions.com/guidePDF

- *Before I Go* Conversation Starter Kit
- 10 Best and Worst Things to Say to Someone Who Is Bereaved
- 13 End of Life Plan Questions to Ask Your Lawyer
- 10 Ways to Avoid Procrastinating
- 25 Important Questions to Ask When Planning Your Funeral

General Information

I know many people don't bother looking at things like resources, but I encourage you to do so with this list, as there is so much information out on the internet about this topic and it can be quite overwhelming. Most of the resources here are ones that I have either personally used, or have been used by someone whom I trust, so do yourself a favour and at least start here.

However, this list is by no means exhaustive and I suggest you also refer to local sources of information in your nearest town or city. There are all kinds of local initiatives that are springing up, as more and more people understand how very important this subject is.

Films

- **Dying Wish** – http://www.dyingwishmedia.com
  Documentary about Dr. Michael Miller, an 80-year-old retired surgeon with end-stage terminal cancer and choosing to stop eating and drinking in order not to prolong the dying process. It's very inspiring and worth watching.

- **Departures** (DVD) – http://www.imdb.com/title/tt1069238 (trailer)
  A poignant story set in Japan about a young man whose life is changed when he embarks on a job as an encoffineer, preparing deceased bodies for burial. Very beautiful and sensitively done.

Books

I've read all these books, amongst others, and that's why they're here – I am happy to recommend them.

- *Final Gifts: Understanding the Special Awareness, Needs and Communications of the Dying* by Maggie Callanan and Patricia Kelley. Beautiful insights from true stories into what the dying can teach us who are still living.

- *The Gift of Alzheimer's: Heart and Soul Journey* by Maggie La Tourelle. Maggie outlines the touching spiritual nature of her mother's journey into Alzheimer's.

- *A Year to Live: How to Live This Year As If It Were Your Last* by Stephen Levine.

- *The Tibetan Book of Living and Dying* by Sogyal Rinpoche.

- *Being Mortal: Illness, Medicine and What Matters in the End* by Atul Gawande. Including the famous questions he suggests all dying patients should be asked, before it's too late.

- *On Death and Dying* by Elisabeth Kuebler Ross. A classic.

- *Smoke Gets In Your Eyes (and Other Lessons from the Crematorium)* by Caitlin Doughty. A great read if you're interested in what goes on behind the scenes.

- *How We Die: Reflections on Life's Final Chapters* by Sherwin B Nuland.

- *On Children and Death* by Elisabeth Kuebler Ross.

- *Who Dies?* by Stephen Levine.

- *Born to Be Free* by Jac O'Keeffe. A great outline of how non-duality principles are behind what we think life is about.

- *Dying to be Me* by Anita Moorjani.

- *The New Natural Death Handbook* by Nicholas Albery, Stephanie Wienrich. Full of useful information, no matter where you are based.

- *The Handbook for Mortals: Guidance for People Facing Serious Illness* by J. Lynn, J. Harrold and J. Schuster.

- *Overcoming the Fear of Death: Through Each of the 4 Main Belief Systems* by Kelvin H. Chin.

- *The Grief Recovery Handbook: The Action Program for Moving Through Death, Divorce and Other Losses* by James and Friedman. If you're going to read just one book to help you with grieving, then this is it.

- *Kicking the Bucket List: 100 Downsizing & Organizing Things to Do Before You Die* by Gail Rubins. Very comprehensive. Dip in and find an area you need to deal with, and take care of it.

- *A Better Way of Dying* by Jeanne and Eileen Fitzpatrick. Sets out very honestly the options available when coming towards the end of life.

Websites and Organizations

Before I Go Solutions (worldwide) – www.beforeigosolutions.com
Support, advice, books, workshops, trainings to help you and others design and create end of life plans. Particularly useful is the free *Before I Go* quiz: How Well-Prepared Are You? Some short but pertinent questions from the workbook to get you thinking about what you need to take care of.

The Natural Death Centre (UK) – www.naturaldeath.org.uk
Full of resources. You can print out a card here to keep in your wallet with regard to your Living Will or Advance Care Directive.

Compassion In Dying (UK) – https://compassionindying.org.uk
Lots of useful resources including reading matter, advance directives and info with regard to wills.

Dying Matters (UK) – https://www.dyingmatters.org
A coalition for England and Wales, providing lots of useful resources.

Final Fling (Scotland) – https://www.finalfling.com
Online resources for you to complete; similar information as is in the *Before I Go Workbook*.

Once I've Gone (UK) – https://onceivegone.com
Resources to help celebrate life and death.

Seven Ponds (USA) – http://sevenponds.com
All end of life resources.

The Order of the Good Death (USA)
– http://www.orderofthegooddeath.com
Funny, uplifting and unusual site. Some fascinating reading matter.

The Groundswell Project (AUS)
– http://www.thegroundswellproject.com
Lots of different ongoing and creative projects to do with end of life.

CHAPTER 4: TALKING ABOUT DEATH

Death Cafes – http://deathcafe.com
> Death Cafes are a movement where people gather together over tea/coffee and cake to talk about anything to do with death.

Let's Talk About Death Over Dinner – www://deathoverdinner.org
> This USA site asks you to complete a few questions about who you'd have for this kind of dinner, and then emails you with suggested text and ideas about how to conduct it.

Conversation Starter Project – https://theconversationproject.org
> Other ways to consider having a conversation and how to do it. US-based.

Compassion in Dying, Starting a Conversation – https://compassionindying.org.uk
> Illustrated booklet. Look under the Info Library heading. UK-based.

Before I Go **Conversation Starter Kit** – https://www.beforeigosolutions.com/guidePDF
> How to prepare for a conversation, what to say, and how to keep going with it.

CHAPTER 5: GRIEF AND BEREAVEMENT

There are many sources of support, including professional advice and support, for bereaved people, and almost definitely a Facebook group or other organization for the particular kind of bereavement that has been suffered. Search for this in your locality, and also for local organizations offering grief counselling.

Gifted By Grief: A True Story of Cancer, Loss and Rebirth – www.giftedbygrief.com
> Jane's site of her book. Includes free information to help you release your grief and feel better in the moment. Available on Amazon and this site.

Life After Death: Six Steps to Improve Support in Bereavement (PDF) – https://www.dyingmatters.org
> Look under Resources. Helpful information about what needs to change at a governmental level. UK-based.

Bereavement Advice (UK) – https://bereavementadvice.org
> Good practical help for when someone dies.

For Stopping Direct Mail for Deceased People (UK)
– https://www.thebereavementregister.org.uk
For stopping direct mail coming to deceased people.

Empathy Cards and Gifts for When People Are Ill
– https://www.notanotherbunchofflowers.com
– http://www.treeol.co.uk

The Grief Recovery Method
– https://www.griefrecoverymethod.com
This organization also publishes a book of the same name, which I highly recommend. Based in the US and UK.

Airlines Bereavement Fares

If you need to travel or adjust travel plans in relation to a bereavement, it is worth checking if your airline offers bereavement fares.

Citizens Advice Bureaux (UK)

Check with your local office for relevant local and national information on dying, death and grief.

CHAPTER 6: AGEING WITHOUT CHILDREN

Ageing Without Children – https://awoc.org
UK-based site full of useful information regardless of what country you are based in.

CHAPTER 7: WHAT IS A BODY?

One Thought Organisation – http://onethought.com
Mara Gleason has written one of the best books on this I have read for organizations: *One Thought Changes Everything*. A good place to start from.

Eckhart Tolle – https://www.eckharttolle.com
Author and spiritual teacher. Awaken to a life of purpose and presence (that includes death).

Jac O'Keeffe – https://jac-okeeffe.com
Jac was the main person in the non-duality field who facilitated so much of my fresh understanding of what thoughts are, and ultimately who we are – that being much more than a body.

Ramana Maharshi – https://www.sriramanamaharshi.org
For everything to do with this spiritual teacher.

CHAPTER 9: LOOKING AFTER THE LEGALS AND FINANCIALS

Charities

Remember to check your favourite charity to see if they offer a will writing option.

Wills UK (Free or low-cost templates)

Law Depot – https://www.lawdepot.co.uk
(England, Wales, Northern Ireland)
Scottish Wills (SCOTLAND) – http://www.scottishwills.com
Which? Magazine (UK) – http://wills.which.co.uk/whichwills
For affordable and easy to follow wills and other legal documents.
Farewill (UK, WALES) – https://farewill.com
Low-cost online and friendly service with professionals on hand.

Power of Attorney

Office of Public Guardian (UK) – https://www.gov.uk/government
/organisations/office-of-the-public-guardian
Very helpful staff and a relatively straightforward procedure for
registering your power of attorney.
On-line legal office (UK) - http://www.mylawyer.co.uk
Which? Magazine (UK) – http://wills.which.co.uk/whichwills
/index.cfm? event =base:poaselector
Anticipatory Care Planning (Scotland/UK) – https://www.youtube.com
/watch?v=UkIQTUpbwbU
Wills and Power of Attorney (USA) – https://www.gyst.com/local
Useful site with resources for wills, insurance, and advance directives
for all the different states, including free downloadable forms
applicable to each state.
US Legal (USA) – http://www.uslegalforms.com/livingwills
Another site with living will information for each different state.
National POLST Paradigm (USA) – http://polst.org
A POLST is a form in the USA that summarizes the patient's wishes
in the form of medical orders, and is only for individuals with a
serious illness or advanced frailty near the end of life.

Everplans – https://www.everplans.com
  Comprehensive offering of all kinds of services for end of life matters.
Canada Wills – http://www.canadawills.com
  Free will templates.

Advance Directives (Living Wills, Advance Decisions, Advance Healthcare Decisions)

United Kingdom

AD Assistance – http://adassistance.org.uk
  Excellent site with suggested wording for particular situations
  and adaptable templates. Will help you no matter what country
  you are in.
Compassion in Dying – http://compassionindying.org.uk/library
  /advance-decision-pack
  A national information service helping you understand your legal
  rights and choices when making decisions about your treatment and
  care. You can print off an AD pack, or complete it online.
Differences between AD's and welfare power of attorney
  – https://bit.ly/2HuGWbM
  A useful article.
Green Cross Scheme
  One example of this can be found at https://www.torbayandsouth
  devon.nhs.uk/uploads/message-in-a-bottle-scheme.pdf

United States

Vital Decisions – http://www.vitaldecisions.net
  For putting end of life health care plans in place.
Good End of Life – http://www.goodendoflife.com
  Basic printable worksheets that cover a plan, your advocates, hospital
  readiness, caregiving guidelines and last words. Plus an excellent
  TED talk: https://bit.ly/2Kj6Kp5
Making a video testimonial – videodirectives.com

Financial Affairs

Savings Expert – https://www.moneysavingexpert.com/family/death-plan
  Article on financial checks that need to be made for your end of life
  plan.

Decluttering – search for local clutter clearance experts, as they will often offer a service where they visit and help you organize and clear your stuff.

CHAPTER 12: LAST DAYS' WISHES

Threshold Choir – http://thresholdchoir.org
For singing at the side of a dying person.

Playlist for Life – www.playlistforlife.org.uk
Created for those with dementia, this site can be used by anyone wanting to create a personal playlist.

Death Doulas

Also known as soul midwives, these are people trained to assist in the dying process. Search in your own country or state for what is being offered there first.

Living Well, Dying Well (UK) – http://www.lwdwtraining.uk
International End of Life Doula Association (USA) – http://inelda.org

Pets

The Cinnamon Trust (UK) – http://www.cinnamon.org.uk
an organization that helps to take care of pets belonging to dying or deceased people
Petfinder (USA) https://www.petfinder.com
works state-wide to find homes for those pets that need adopted

Caring for bodies at home

Pushing Up the Daisies (Scotland) – http://pushingupthedaisies.org.uk
Natural Death (England and Wales) – http://www.naturaldeath.org.uk
/index.php?page =diy-funerals
Crossings.net (USA) – http://crossings.net/resourceguide030109.pdf
A useful guide.

Hospice UK

In the UK these are specific places into which a patient is admitted. Best to search on the internet for your closest one and visit them well in advance of when you think it might be needed. Each hospice will have their own way of doing things. Volunteering there will also give you a better insight into how they work.

Hospice USA

Hospice in America refers to a type of end of life care often provided at home. Under hospice, medical and social services are supplied to patients and their families by an interdisciplinary team of professional providers and volunteers, who take a patient-directed approach to managing illness. You need to find out what is available in your particular state.

CHAPTER 13: FOR SMALL BUSINESS OWNERS

Federation of Small Businesses (UK) – http://www.fsb.org.uk
National Federation of Independent Business (USA)
    – http://www.nfib. com
FamilyBusinessPlace.com – https://familybusinessplace.com
    Some excellent resources for family businesses everywhere.

CHAPTER 15: AFTER DEATH

Cryomation – http://irtl.co.uk
Embalming – https://bit.ly/2jda7S5
    Useful US-based article asking this very question.
Body Donation UK – https://www.hta.gov.uk/faqs/body-donation-faqs
    For questions about this, including the local medical establishments accepting bodies. Consent forms are also available here, which allow you to clearly state what you want.

Organ Donation

England and Wales - https://www.organdonation.nhs.uk
Scotland - http://www.organdonationscotland.org
Northern Ireland - https://www.organdonationni.info
USA - https://organdonor.gov/index.html

Cremation

United Kingdom

http://www.naturaldeath.org.uk/index.php?page=cremation

United States

http://www.cremationassociation.org
http://www.us-funerals.com
https://www.neptunesociety.com (for affordable cremations)

Direct Disposal

There are more and more of these services popping up every day. Check your local information for the nearest to you. Here is a good description:

Good Funeral Guide (UK) – https://www.goodfuneralguide.co.uk/what
-do-you-pay-for-2
Resomation – http://resomation.com
Promession – http://www.cryonics.org

Home Burial

Natural Death (UK) – http://www.naturaldeath.org.uk/index.php?
page =home-burial
Burial Laws (USA) – http://coeio.com/burial-laws-state
A site giving burial laws by state. Double check these with your your local sources.

Burial at Sea

License (UK)– https://www.gov.uk/guidance/how-to-get-a-licence-for-a
-burial-at-sea-in-england
Permits (USA) – https://www.epa.gov/ocean-dumping/burial-sea
(has a good Q & A section)

Funerals

You are best to research these locally, but the resources below give excellent general information. Look at these first, then you can refine your local search.

Good Funeral Guide (UK) – http://www.goodfuneralguide.co.uk
For all matters funereal.
Natural Death Centre (UK) – http://www.naturaldeath.org.uk
Excellent site that promotes choice in all matters of dying and death. They also run the Association of Natural Burial Grounds.

Do-It-Yourself Funerals

Natural Death (England) – http://www.naturaldeath.org.uk
Pushing up the Daisies (Scotland) – http://pushingupthedaisies.org.uk
Crossings (USA) – http://crossings.net/resourceguide030109.pdf
    A manual for home funeral care.
DIY Coffins – http://www.leedam.com/uploads/1/3/9/7/13978721
    /basic-diy-coffin-plans.pdf
    Plans to enable you to make your own coffin or casket.

Home Funerals

Good Funeral Guide (UK) – http://www.goodfuneralguide.co.uk/find-a
    -funeral-director/do-it-all-yourself
Home Funeral Network (UK) – http://www.homefuneralnetwork.org.uk
Final Passages (USA) – http://finalpassages.org
    Just one of many sites devoted to this way of doing funerals.

Obituaries/Eulogies

Celebrancy: As this is a growing area, new initiatives are being developed all the time, so search for something local or try any of these sites:

United Kingdom

https://www.interfaithfoundation.org
https://www.thecelebrantdirectory.com
http://www.alternativeceremony.org
https://humanism.org.uk

United States

https://www.onespiritinterfaith.org
http://www.celebrantinstitute.org
https://americanhumanist.org

CHAPTER 16: YOUR DIGITAL LIFE

Passwords and Privacy

Some of the current popular methods to safely secure and remember them:
https://1password.com
https://www.lastpass.com
https://keepass.info

Social Media

Google your particular social media site with search terms such as deceased members, what to do when someone dies, memorialized account and you will be directed to the most up-to-date information.

Endnotes

• • • • • •

INTRODUCTION

1   http://theconversationproject.org/wp-content/uploads/2017/02
/ConversationProject-ConvoStarterKit-English.pdf

CHAPTER 1: WHY NOW?

2   https://www.zanebenefits.com/blog/the-cost-of-healthcare-in-america

3   https://www.mariecurie.org.uk/globalassets/media/documents
/commissioning-our-services/publications/understanding-cost-end
-life-care-different-settingspdf

CHAPTER 3: WHY BOTHER?

4   Dying Matters British Social Attitudes Survey http://www.dying
matters.org/sites/default/files/BSA30_Full_Report.pdf

5   http://news.gallup.com/poll/191651/majority-not.aspx

6   https://compassionindying.org.uk/library/plan-well-die-well

CHAPTER 6: AGEING WITHOUT CHILDREN

7   https://www.caregiver.org/caregiver-statistics-demographics

8   https://awoc.org

CHAPTER 7: WHAT IS A BODY?

9   From Gifted By Grief: A True Story of Cancer, Loss and Rebirth. By
Jane Duncan Rogers. Living Well Publications. www.giftedbygrief.com

10   https://www.brainyquote.com/quotes/quotes/r/ramanamaha
753135.html

11   http://www.nytimes.com/1994/06/12/arts/dennis-potter-s-last
-interview-on-nowness-and-his-work.html?pagewanted=all

CHAPTER 9: LOOKING AFTER THE LEGALS

12   https://www.willaid.org.uk

13   https://compassionindying.org.uk/library/plan-well-die-well

14   https://www.theguardian.com/healthcare-network/2016/feb/03
     /casualty-cpr-fails-cancer-doctors-let-patients-die

15   https://www.sciencedaily.com/releases/2015/06/150630135103.htm

16   http://www.yorkshirepost.co.uk/news/analysis/a-life-and-death-battle
     -that-exposes-the-choices-we-all-may-have-to-make-1-6388422

CHAPTER 12: LAST DAYS WISHES

17   https://www.sueryder.org/~/media/files/about-us/a-time-and-a-place
     -sue-ryder.ashx

18   https://palliative.stanford.edu/home-hospice-home-care-of-the-dying
     -patient/where-do-americans-die

CHAPTER 13: SMALL BUSINESSES

19   http://www.thisismoney.co.uk/money/smallbusiness/article-2336898
     /What-happen-business-die.html

CHAPTER 15: FOR AFTER DEATH

20   https://en.wikipedia.org/wiki/Embalming

21   https://yougov.co.uk/news/2016/08/16/majority-people-want-be
     -cremated-when-they-die

22   http://www.cremationassociation.org/page/IndustryStatistics

23   http://www.co-operativefuneralcare.co.uk/after-the-funeral/featured
     -articles/help-with-accounts-online

CHAPTER 18: YOUR DIGITAL LIFE

24   https://support.google.com/accounts/answer/3036546?hl=en

25   https://www.facebook.com/help/1506822589577997

Index

••••••

Acknowledgements

• • • • • •

There have been many people involved in the writing of this Guide, not to mention the hundreds who have bought the workbook, attended the *Before I Go* courses in their various formats, and those who are on my mailing list. A huge thank you to all of them, some of whom have their stories in this Guide.

Thank you also to the many in the Findhorn Foundation Community, particularly those involved with Adriana's death (Francine, Pat and Heleen).

Joanna Legard and Ian Shearer were worthy readers of the manuscript, pointing out errors, and where I had got my ideas mixed up. A huge thanks also to those who have endorsed it: Robert Holden, Barbara Chalmers, Tiffany Jane Crossara, Phyllida Anam-Aire, William Bloom, Claire Henry.

The directors of *Before I Go Solutions* ® have been a source of great support: Cornelia Featherstone, Liz Egan, Ian Shearer, and Ray Martin.

Legal advice was freely given and gratefully received from Alua Arthur, Attorney and End of Life Planner at **www.goingwithgrace.com** with regard to the USA, Hilary Peppiette, solicitor and death doula in Scotland, and Jane Cassell of **http://www.jcwillsandprobate.co.uk/** in England.

Colleagues all over the world have been a source of inspiration and guidance, specifically Patty Burgess Brecht of Doing Death Differently, Sherry Richert Belul of Simply Celebrate, Alina Vincent of Business Success Edge, Tracey Muirhead of the School of Social Entrepreneurs, Kelly Jo Murphy of JVIC, Kate Clark of Pushing Up the Daisies, and Lorraine Porter of the Investing Women network.

Many people I met through Facebook have also helped, including Sarah Sinciewicz, Sarah Weller, Tiffany Jane Crossara, Lucy Coulbert, Gail Rubin, Karen Wyatt, Beate Scheenberg and all those in the *Before I Go* Facebook group. Other Facebook groups have also been a source of inspiration and support.

Editors Sabine Weeke and Michael Hawkins of Findhorn Press have been a patient source of wise words and inspiration. Thank you!

About the Author

· · · · · ·

Jane Duncan Rogers is founder of *Before I Go Solutions*®, a not-for-profit social enterprise that educates people to become more at ease with dying, death and grief, through helping them design and create good end of life plans.

Having been in the field of psychotherapy and personal growth for 25 years, Jane is author of *Gifted By Grief: A True Story of Cancer, Loss and Rebirth*. She lives near the Findhorn Foundation community in Scotland, UK, and loves to walk, meditate and sing (when she's not reading or writing). For more information or to contact her see: https://beforeigosolutions.com

Also of Interest

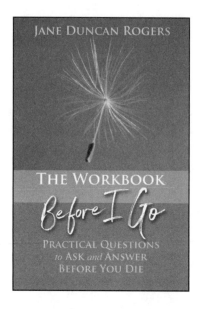

The Before I Go Workbook
by Jane Duncan Rogers

THE BEFORE I GO WORKBOOK can be used as a companion to this guide, outlining over 140 questions that provide support for completing your end of life plan.

What do you want done with your body after your death? How do you want it dressed? What do you want done with your social media presence? Do you want to write your own eulogy? Who would know your passwords? Addressing these and other questions in time helps to give yourself peace of mind and ensure your relatives have no need to disagree, worry or spend extra time and money sorting things out after the end of your life.

Available now as a downloadable and fillable PDF, for you to print out or complete on your device from **www.beforeigosolutions.com**. Coming as a print copy soon.

Gifted By Grief
by Jane Duncan Rogers

HAVING HAD NO CHILDREN, Jane's greatest fear comes true when she is left alone in the world after her husband, Philip, dies from stomach cancer. Gifted by Grief is the story of how they cope with the diagnosis and what emerges for her after he dies. She describes how, two and a half years on, after all the grief and loss, she ends up stating something she would never have believed was possible: she is grateful for the loss of her husband.

Musings about the meaning of life and death, including excerpts from Philip's blog posts and Jane's journal entries at the time, are interwoven with funny, poignant and insightful stories. This gives a unique insight into one of the most challenging times a relationship can face.

Filled with golden nuggets of wisdom for the reader to pick up and use as they wish, this book introduces the idea that within all grief there is a gift awaiting discovery. An excellent bereavement book, for those suffering grief from any cause, and also for those who want to support friends or family members who have been bereaved.

978-0-95374-031-4

FINDHORN PRESS

Life-Changing Books

Learn more about us and our books at
www.findhornpress.com

For information on the Findhorn Foundation:
www.findhorn.org

31901063242707